# ANTIQUES ROADSHOW

## 40 YEARS OF GREAT FINDS

# ANTIQUES ROADSHOW

## 40 YEARS OF GREAT FINDS

Paul Atterbury & Marc Allum

WILLIAM
COLLINS

William Collins
An imprint of HarperCollinsPublishers
1 London Bridge Street
London SE1 9GF

**WilliamCollinsBooks.com**

First published in Great Britain by William Collins in 2017

22 21 20 19 18 17
10 9 8 7 6 5 4 3 2 1

ISBN 978-0-00-826763-6

Publishing Director: Myles Archibald
Senior Editor: Julia Koppitz
Edited and designed by Guy Croton Publishing Services, Maidstone, Kent


Colour reproduction by Born Group
Printed and bound in Germany by Mohn Media

*Frontispiece: a typical indoor* Roadshow *day in the early 1980s.*

# CONTENTS

Introduction  8–15

A William Burges bottle  16–19
A Sioux Warrior bronze  20–21
Ozzy the owl  24–7
A Foujita painting  28–9
A Richard Dadd painting  30–3
An Album of Filipino watercolours  36–7
Paul Storr salts  38–41
A Renaissance gold plaque  42–3
A Delftware Turk's head  44–7
A pair of Regency peat buckets  50–51
A William Orpen portrait  52–5
A Churchill cigar  56–7
A Steiff *Titanic* bear  58–61
A Waterloo chest  62–3
The credenza story  64–5
A Francis Souza painting  66–7
Mughal bracelets  68–9
Scott expedition photographs  72–5
The Blue John  76–7
Queen Anne's travelling chest  78–81
Buffalo Bill's gloves  82–3
An Alma-Tadema portrait  86–9
A cold-painted bronze parrot  90–1
Van Dyck portrait  92–5
A Stuart table casket  98–9
Henry Moore letters  100–3
A Märklin tinplate biplane  104–5
The Cottingley fairies  106–9
Scrimshaw carvers  110–11
Newspaper posters  112–13
Beatrix Potter drawings  114–17

'The Winner' enamel advertising sign  118–19
The Keel of *Endeavour*  122–3
Sunbeam-Talbot 90 Rally car  124–5
*Carpathia* memorabilia  126–7
A Leica II Luxus camera  128–31
A Terry Frost portrait  134–5
Marc Bolan's Gibson 'Flying V' guitar  136–9
Graham Sutherland painting  140–1
A Lalique vase  142–5
Dambusters' panda mascot  148–9
A plane spotter's notebooks  150–3
A William Burges brooch  154–5
A stump work box  156–9
*Titanic* letter  160–1
A Saxon gold ring  164–5
A Tourmaline ring  166–7
A silver duck claret jug  168–9
The refuse tip jewellery  170–1
An English marquetry commode  174–5
Margaret James, poster designer  176–9
A William Kent style table  180–1
An Audemars Piguet watch  184–5
An eighteenth-century dress  186–9
Status Quo tapestry  190–1
Lawrence of Arabia's watch  192–3
A diamond butterfly brooch  194–5
A Steiff Clown bear  198–9
The Hiroshima Bowls  200–1
The Great Train Robbers' *Monopoly* set  202–3
A Thomas Telford gate  204–5
A Yuan bronze vase  206–7
A bizarre fishing rod  208–9

A Japonisme Gem  210–11
A Suffragette medal  214–17
A Lindner portrait  218–19
Fiji bulibuli club  220–3
The Tory loo seat  226–7
A Dolls' house  228–31
An Apothecary cabinet  232–3
A Shakespeare notebook  234–7
Banksy lovers  240–3
An English Rose kitchen  244–5
JFK's flying jacket  246–7
Rommel's cigarette packet  248–51
Old Testament figures  252–3
Jean Dupas posters  254–5
A Chinese armorial dish  256–7
A Frodsham mantel clock  258–9
A Cartier wristwatch  260–1
Mrs Ambrose's punch pot  262–3
Martinware collection  264–7
Lloyd's Patriotic Fund sword  268–9

Cromwell's funeral flag  272–5
Jane Austen's cup-and-ball  276–7
The Crawley silver  278–9
A George Richmond miniature  280–1
A caravan planned by a P.O.W.  282–5
'May the Force'  286–7
An L. S. Lowry painting  288–9
Bull's head stirrup cups  290–1
Dickin medals  292–3
A Lewis Carroll collection  294–5
An Indian portrait  296–7
An Early doll  298–9
A Maria Heathcote portrait  300–1
A Weird glass  302–3
Special programmes  306–13

Index  316–18
Picture credits  319
Acknowledgements  320

*Familiar Roadshow faces, as they were.* CLOCKWISE: *David Battie, Eric Knowles, Lars Tharp and Henry Sandon.*

# INTRODUCTION

On 17 May 1977, a group of antiques experts and a BBC production team came together in Hereford's town hall to make a pilot programme for a possible new series, to be called the *Antiques Roadshow*. The idea was simple. Members of the public would be encouraged to bring their own objects for identification, discussion and valuation to a team of experts assembled for the purpose in a large public space, with television crews standing by to film the best bits. On paper, it seemed like a good idea, but no one knew on that May morning whether it would work or not.

The inspiration had come from one of the regular valuation days organised by auction houses, whereby members of the public could bring things along for a free valuation, as a means of generating business. One such occasion was visited by a production team from BBC Bristol, and the idea of developing it into a public event that could also be a television programme was born. At the planning stage, advice was sought from Sotheby's by BBC Bristol. For the programme, however, there was to be no commercial agenda.

## A PROGRAMME IS COMMISSIONED

Plans were drawn up, Hereford town hall and the expert team were booked, and the event was widely publicised, with the offer of free transport for large pieces of furniture and other items that could not easily be carried by their owners.

A programme about antiques was not a new idea for the BBC. *Talking about Antiques*, a radio programme presented by Bernard Price, had enjoyed long-lasting success in the 1960s. In 1965 *Going for a Song*, presented by Max Robertson and, later, *Collectors'World*, first broadcast in 1970 and presented by Hugh Scully, brought antiques successfully onto the television screen. All these programmes generated a large mailbox from listeners and viewers keen to find out about their own objects, and so a programme designed to help those people do just that was considered to stand a good chance of success. Thus, the pilot for the *Antiques Roadshow* was commissioned.

A key figure was, of course, Arthur Negus. After a long and successful career as a valuer and furniture expert with a Gloucestershire firm of auctioneers, Arthur started a new life as a television personality at the age of 62, when he joined the panel of experts on *Going for a Song*. He was an immediate success, thanks to his relaxed manner and West Country accent, and quickly became the face of antiques on television. Needless to say, Arthur Negus was at the

At Castle Howard in July 2017, to mark the Roadshow's 40th anniversary, a special guest was Bruce Parker, the show's first presenter, seen here with Fiona Bruce.

*Angela Rippon, the presenter for the Roadshow's second and third series, with Arthur Negus, the programme's most famous expert in the early days.*

heart of the team of experts assembled by the BBC for the *Antiques Roadshow* pilot, although it is important to remember that he was never the programme's presenter.

On that May day in Hereford, the *Roadshow* quickly developed the winning formula, format, shape and style that it was broadly to follow for the next forty years. In a programme nominally about objects and their values, it soon became apparent that it could also be about their owners. As Hugh Scully once said: '*The programme is a cameo of the British character and its foibles, idiosyncrasies and eccentricities. It is the people that we most readily remember. They are the* Antiques Roadshow. *They give it the colour, charm, interest, anecdote and humour that delight us on Sunday evenings. We enjoy their happiness. We share their hopes. We feel their disappointments.*'

*In 1996 the* Roadshow *was awarded a BAFTA, the Lew Grade Award for a Significant and Popular Television Programme. Hugh Scully and Christopher Lewis, Executive Producer at the time, show off the award.*

Pilot programmes are rarely transmitted, but that first experimental show at Hereford went so well that it was included in the first series, once it had been commissioned. Between April and August 1978, the *Roadshow* visited Bedworth, Yeovil, Newbury, Northallerton, Buxton, Perth and Mold, setting a pattern, and a geographical spread, that has remained much the same ever since. As the *Roadshow*'s popularity grew, so more filming locations were steadily added. By 1986 it had risen to twelve and by 1997 to twenty five, with a filming season that ran from 16 April 1997 to 19 March 1998. The next series started filming just over a month later, on 23 April 1998. More recently, the *Roadshow*'s filming schedule has settled at twelve episodes each year, but with two programmes being made at each location. Also consistent has been the

ABOVE: *Michael Aspel fronted the* Roadshow *for eight years, hosting 200 episodes between the years 2000 and 2008.* OPPOSITE: *Fiona Bruce has been presenting the* Roadshow *since 2008.*

programme's popularity and, forty years on from that day in Hereford, the *Roadshow* continues to attract on the day between 1,500 and 4,500 people keen to queue for hours for the chance to discuss their objects with the team of experts. For the first twenty or so years, the *Roadshow* was filmed from indoor locations such as sports halls and civic centres. In the late 1990s, the first outdoor locations appeared and, since then, the *Roadshow*'s locations have generally been both outdoors and at places of architectural or historic interest.

## A HARD-WORKING PROGRAMME

The *Roadshow*'s core values have never changed. All objects, and their owners, are treated equally, regardless of the value. On the day, the team may assess and discuss between 7,000 and 12,000 objects, of which around fifty will be filmed and the experts will see everyone who comes in to the location before the entry deadline, which is usually 4.30pm. After that, everyone who has made it into the location before the deadline will be seen, and so the experts have a long day, usually starting at around 9am and finishing at any time between 5pm and 7pm, depending on the numbers present. The actual filming starts at 9.30am and finishes at 7pm. There can be no previewing of the objects, because there is no way of knowing in advance what the public are going to bring in. There is no 'B' team to deal with the less valuable or interesting objects. There is only one team, and it sees everything and everybody. When it comes to the filming, there are no rehearsals or run-throughs. Every item is filmed as live, but these live conversations will be edited into the items that are included in the transmitted programme. Finally, the *Roadshow* is not only a flagship programme for the BBC, but is also a major public event and a classic example of traditional public service broadcasting.

During its forty years, five people have presented the *Roadshow*. The first series was introduced by Bruce Parker, a familiar journalist and presenter for BBC South. For the second and third series he was replaced by Angela Rippon, then a nationally known news presenter, keen to develop her career in new directions. For series four, in 1981, Hugh Scully took the helm – a presenter much closer in both interests and experience to the world of art and antiques – and he was to remain the face of the *Roadshow* until 2000. Above all else, he appreciated the *Roadshow*'s special quality: '*It is a programme that has maintained its freshness without having to make any drastic changes, purely because of the unpredictable nature of the event.*' Michael Aspel, who took over the presenter's baton from Hugh, agreed. '*Having spent many years on programmes where every moment of the recording is planned, it is very exciting to approach a day on the* Roadshow *with absolutely no idea*

*Outdoor* Roadshows *started in the late 1990s, and since then scenes like this have come to define the modern programme.*

of what is going to happen. The people and their objects make the programme, and we react accordingly.' In 2008, Fiona Bruce took the helm, and she has been at the heart of the *Roadshow* ever since. Famous for her hands-on approach, Fiona also loves the programme's particular quality: '*It's all spontaneous and entirely unpredictable.*'

## THE ATTRIBUTES OF A ROADSHOW EXPERT

From that small band of experts recruited for that pilot programme in Hereford has grown a remarkable team of knowledgeable and enthusiastic men and women drawn from all areas of the world of art and antiques. An expert on the *Roadshow* has to possess several attributes. Knowledge, and the ability to present that knowledge in an accessible manner is key, but they also have to be great team players and always ready to share their knowledge. They must have great patience and be willing to talk for hours to owners about their objects, not all of which will be very exciting. In short, they should like people and enjoy engaging with them. They must remain friendly and enthusiastic throughout a long and sometime challenging day, often with very few breaks. Most importantly, they have to be ambassadors for the programme and the BBC. At most *Roadshows* there will be a team of twenty to twenty-five experts on duty, covering all the disciplines, but the make-up of the team will vary from show to show.

Today, the *Roadshow* has around fifty-six experts in the team, but this number has never been consistent. In the days when more programmes were filmed for each series, the team reached over eighty to ensure that every discipline could be fully represented at each event. In the current team there is one expert, David Battie, who was present at that first Hereford programme, but many others joined soon after. Indeed, the *Roadshow* is remarkable for the longevity of its experts, with well over half the team having served twenty years or more. At the same time, new experts join each year, usually recruited either by the production team or by experts who sometimes act as informal talent scouts.

## MOVING WITH THE TIMES

During its long life, the *Roadshow* has had three executive producers: Robin Drake; Christopher Lewis; and Simon Shaw. Longevity has also been a feature of the programme's production team, with many working on the show for years. Making the *Roadshow* is an immensely complex process, and planning can take months or even years. Every show is dependent upon the great skills of the production, technical and support teams.

There have been changes during the last forty years, but these have generally been introduced in a gentle and unobtrusive way. Most obvious are the titles. Having been changed or developed every few years, these have now gone through several versions. For the first few years, the theme music was an electronic version of Bach's Third Brandenberg Concerto, but this was replaced by the now globally familiar tune, a specially commissioned piece written by Paul Reade and Tim Gibson. The most important change has been a gradual shift in emphasis away from the antiques and their values towards the owners and their stories. This is partly reflective of significant changes in the world of antiques itself, as the interest in traditional antiques diminishes, replaced by new enthusiasms for more modern items. The *Roadshow* has now entertained more than two generations of viewers, and the tastes of the modern viewer are not the same as those who watched the programme in the late 1970s and 1980s. In its own leisurely way, the *Antiques Roadshow* has had to move with the times.

# A WILLIAM BURGES
# BOTTLE

---

*'I was very lucky to be able to film something so important at a relatively early stage in my* Roadshow *career. It is still one of the best things I have ever seen.'*

Paul Atterbury

Near the end of a busy day in October 1996 at the Embassy Centre in Skegness, Lincolnshire, Paul Atterbury had taken a break from his table to have a cup of tea in the Centre's restaurant. As he sat down, one of the show's receptionists came over to him clutching a shopping basket in which lay a silver-mounted bottle. For Paul, it was a moment of magic, as he knew at once that he was looking at a long-lost treasure designed by the great Victorian architect, William Burges.

Paul rushed back to the hall to show the bottle to his friend, colleague and fellow Victorian enthusiast David Battie, and they agreed at once that it had to be filmed. Schedules, which at that point in the day were full as usual, were rearranged and, unusually, it was agreed that Paul and David should film it together, in conversation with the owner.

## WILLIAM BURGES

A bizarre and eccentric figure, William Burges (1827–1881), was one of the greatest architect/ designers of the latter part of the Victorian period. Drawing inspiration from many sources – including High Gothic and Tudor styles, French illuminated manuscripts, the Middle East and various worlds of myth and fantasy – Burges created extraordinary buildings and interiors, along with furniture, metalwork, jewellery and wallpapers. His great friend and major client was John Crichton-Stuart, the 3rd Marquess of Bute, and then one of the richest men in Britain, for whom he created Castell Coch near Cardiff, and extravagantly rebuilt Cardiff Castle. Burges was a consummate colourist and his legacy is a Victorian vision of magnificent splendour and richness.

Burges is known to have designed a wide range of decorative objects in silver and other metals, mostly for his own use at his extraordinary house in Melbury Road, West London, which was full of such treasures. Many are now lost, though they were recorded in a series of photographs taken in the 1880s and mounted in an album that is now in the Victoria & Albert Museum in London.

Paul and David were able to establish quite quickly that this bottle was one of those lost pieces, not seen for over a hundred years. The bottle itself, only about seven inches high, is

*Hugh Scully, David Battie and Paul Atterbury after filming the William Burges bottle.*

eighteenth century Chinese porcelain with a coffee-coloured glaze, in itself not exceptional but made so by Burges' mounts – organic tendrils in jewel-mounted gilded silver – that encase it. The cover is crowned with a pearl-set spider and Burges' name and the date, 1864, are carried on a band of enamel around the base. In Europe, the tradition of enriching Chinese porcelain with jewelled mounts goes back to the Elizabethan era, an historical reference typical of Burges.

## AN EXTRAORDINARY FIND

During the filming, the lady owner was asked about the background to the bottle. All she knew was that her father, a travelling salesman, had bought it in about 1950 from an antique shop somewhere along the Great North Road. She explained that her father, who had an extraordinary eye and great curiosity, often came home with strange things that he had found on his travels.

She remembered that the bottle was one of the most unusual things he found and that he had paid £100 for it, which at the time had seemed a huge amount of money. Having recovered from her shock at the cost, she had forgotten about it, only finding it again after her father's death.

She revealed that she had never looked at it in detail and had not seen the signature on the enamel band. When it was pointed out to her, she said it meant nothing to her as she had never heard of Burges. Bringing it to the *Roadshow* had been a last-minute decision, and she said she had very nearly not bothered to come.

## AN AUCTION-STYLE VALUATION

Paul and David did the valuation in the form of an auction, taking it in turns to bid until the price reached £30,000. The owner was amazed, but said immediately that it was going back in the sideboard where it lived. Since then, it has never been seen again. Attempts to trace the owner and the bottle during the preparation of this book were unsuccessful. It has not appeared on the market, although similar metalwork by Burges has been sold. It would be a tragedy if this great treasure, lost for a century before its brief *Roadshow* appearance, is now lost again.

Paul still remembers the sense of excitement and discovery when he first saw the bottle lying in the shopping basket. '*I have always loved Victorian design, particularly exceptional things like this. Burges was a genius, staggeringly original in his ideas and his craft. Great metalwork by him so rarely comes onto the market. We have had one other major Burges piece in forty years of the* Roadshow, *a brooch that Geoffrey Munn found. I still feel exactly the same about the bottle, it will always be a highlight of my* Roadshow *life. It was a classic case of being in the right place at the right time. And sharing it with David was a treat, I think we both knew we were very lucky.*'

Today, the William Burges bottle is probably worth £60,000.

# A SIOUX WARRIOR BRONZE

One of the highlights of a rather wet *Roadshow* at Bodnant Gardens, Wales, in 2009 was a powerful equestrian bronze of a Sioux warrior. Furniture specialist Christopher Payne, who has written books about nineteenth century bronzes, was excited to see it, partly because of its rarity and also because it is unusual to find American bronzes of this quality in Britain.

Called *Appeal to the Great Spirit*, and the final sculpture in a series of four equestrian pieces known as the *Epic of the Indian*, it was modelled in 1909 by Cyrus Dallin and cast in Paris. The first of the series, *A Signal of Peace*, was shown in Chicago in 1893; the second *The Medicine Man* in Paris in 1899; the third, *The Protest* in St Louis in 1904; and the fourth, *Appeal*, in Paris in 1909. Born in Utah in 1861, Dallin was a prolific and well-known sculptor who produced over 240 works, many inspired by a view of American history that he shared with Frederick Remington, the other great American sculptor of this period. Dallin grew up with native North American children, developing a great respect for tribal history and culture at a time when that aspect of American history was under threat. The full-size version of *Appeal to the Great Spirit* has stood outside the Museum of Fine Arts in Boston since 1912. In America, there are other full-size versions of what is now seen as Dallin's greatest work. In 1922 a small edition of small versions was issued, with other editions following until Dallin's death in 1944. Since then, this iconic sculpture has been frequently reproduced.

Christopher Payne often picks this as one of his favourite *Roadshow* moments, because the bronze brought to Bodnant was one of the early casts, not a later reproduction. For that reason he valued it between £60,000 and £80,000, knowing that another early cast had sold in New York in 2005 for $120,000. He explained the bronze's powerful message to the owner, namely that the story of native North American culture was being obliterated by the rapid development of industrialised white America, a message that perhaps resonates even more powerfully today. Hence the title – the *Appeal to the Great Spirit* – to save the tribe and all it represents.

The owner knew little about it, having acquired it about ten years earlier from his wife's father, someone he described as '*an eccentric local bank manager whose hobby was marrying wealthy heiresses*'.

# OZZY THE OWL

*'An ordinary slipware mug would have been an exciting find but the figures, like Ozzy, are rarer still, so he really was a very important discovery.'*

Henry Sandon

In September 1989, Northampton's Derngate Centre was the setting for one of the *Roadshow*'s most famous finds – a Staffordshire slipware owl with a detachable head, known ever since as Ozzy the Owl, even though this was the name of the mascot used by Sheffield Wednesday Football Club. The lady owner brought the owl to the *Roadshow* on the bus, and was very taken aback by the excitement it had generated. She could not remember how it had come into the family, only that it had been there for years, first owned by her aunt and then by her mother, and had often been used, without the head, as a flower vase.

## AN IMPORTANT AND DISTINCTIVE DISCOVERY

Slipware is one of the earliest and most distinctive types of British domestic pottery, widely in use throughout the seventeenth century. The technique of decorating ordinary red, brown or buff clays with slip, or liquid clay, in other colours is even older, dating at least from the medieval period. Various decorative techniques, including pouring or dotting the slip onto the surface, scratching designs through the poured slip – a process known as *sgraffito* – and feathering it into swirly patterns with a quill, were all carried out before the pot was fired. When fully decorated, the pot was given a clear, lead glaze.

Slipware was associated with many parts of Britain, including the West Country, Kent, South Wales, the Midlands and Yorkshire, but the main centre of production was Staffordshire. Dishes, bowls, mugs and other domestic wares were made in large quantities by many Staffordshire potters throughout the seventeenth century and into the early years of the eighteenth, often with a distinctive and complex style of slip decoration that makes them readily identifiable. The most famous pieces are large chargers, intricately decorated in raised slip with mottoes and texts, portraits, cross-hatching and other patterns, usually in a complex but appealingly primitive style. Feathering was a favoured Staffordshire technique, creating an intricately patterned surface that looked like marbling. Some Staffordshire slipware potters are known – for example, Thomas Toft – but the majority remain anonymous, including the maker of the owls with their detachable heads. A small number are recorded, mostly in museums, and expert Henry Sandon believes that they all came from the hands of one potter.

During the filming, Henry was barely able to contain his excitement. Clutching the owl to his chest, he said that he had never handled one before. In fact, he seemed quite reluctant to give it back to the owner! He explained how the head could be used as a drinking cup, a type of vessel known in various forms since the Egyptian era. '*Surviving pieces of Staffordshire slipware are rare and desirable, but this little drinking pot – the body would have been used as a jug and the head as a cup – is in feathered slipware, which is even rarer.*' The lady owner, increasingly bemused both by Henry's enthusiasm and what he was telling her, was visibly shocked as he steadily increased the value from £500 to £20,000. '*Well. I never*', was her only response. After the filming, the lady and her owl were sent home in a taxi, accompanied by two policemen, much to the consternation of her mother when she opened the front door.

## BACK TO ITS ROOTS

During the eighteenth and early nineteenth centuries, there was little interest in Staffordshire slipware and it was generally dismissed as peasant pottery. It was not properly appreciated until the 1880s, when the first book about it appeared. Entitled *The Art of the Old English Potter,* it was written by the great French artist and designer L. M. Solon, who worked with Staffordshire ceramics company Mintons from the early 1870s. Since then, high-quality Staffordshire slipware has always been seen as rare and desirable although, unfortunately, fakes have been made since the late Victorian period. However, there was no doubt about Ozzy's authenticity.

Not long after Ozzy's *Roadshow* appearance, the family decided to part with him. He was put up for sale at Phillips auction house in London and sold for £22,000 to an agent acting on behalf of the Potteries Museum in Stoke-on-Trent. So the owl returned home and now lives in a special case in the museum, not far from where he was made in the late seventeenth century. Immediately popular, the owl has become a kind of mascot for the museum, and his presence there has greatly increased the number of visitors. On a couple of occasions since then, Henry Sandon has been reunited with Ozzy and, together, the two revisited Henry's greatest *Roadshow* moment and the show's most famous find. Later, the former owner told Henry that she had used some of the money to help support five orphans in various parts of the world.

# A FOUJITA PAINTING

The *Roadshow*'s first visit to London occurred in 1990, and thousands queued at the recently restored Royal Agricultural Hall in Islington, now the Business Design Centre. On a busy day, one of the most unexpected finds was a painting by the Japanese artist, Tsuguharu Foujita. The owner, a local man, explained that he had been sitting in a café across the road watching the slow progress of the queue when his wife suggested that they collect a painting hanging on the wall at their nearby home and, when the queue had subsided, take it in for an opinion. Philip Hook, one of the painting specialists on duty that day, was delighted they had done so, for it gave him a chance to talk about one of the most interesting paintings he had seen during his *Roadshow* career.

Born in Tokyo in 1866, Foujita trained initially at the city's Imperial Academy of Fine Art. In 1910 he travelled to China and London before settling in Paris in 1913 and living there until his death in 1968. Paris in the 1920s was a turbulent and exciting city, filled with artists and writers from all over the world, and over 100 galleries showed the work of 60,000 artists, many of whom were foreigners. In the cafés of the Left Bank, Foujita could have met painters such as Chagall, Modigliani, Soutine and Picasso, not to mention writers including Ernest Hemingway. It was a period of astonishing creativity, with Paris at the centre of a world that was rapidly establishing the principles and styles of modern art. At first, Foujita painted landscapes, nudes and still-lifes, but he quickly developed his own way of working – a gentle blend of Western and Japanese styles, bringing together Japanese print and Far Eastern painting and calligraphy with Matisse and Picasso.

Philip explained this to the owners and pointed out Foujita's signature in both Japanese and Western script, reflecting his unique position as the most important Japanese artist working in Europe in the twentieth century. Philip dated the painting to around 1920, a time when Foujita's distinctive Franco-Japanese style was just emerging, and he valued it at £50,000, a sum that visibly shocked the owners. At that time, the Japanese market was booming, so the painting might fetch less if sold today.

# A RICHARD DADD
# PAINTING

'*If it is night when you arrive, the effects of light and shadow are something only to be painted, not described... At times the excitement of these scenes has been enough to turn the brain of an ordinary weak-minded person like myself... The moon rose again after some time, and we, having stayed two hours, mounted and rode through the mountains of Engaddi.*'

Richard Dadd, letter to William Powell Frith, 26 November 1842

With all the pressure and excitement of a *Roadshow* day, there is little time for detailed research. Sometimes objects – most frequently paintings – have been filmed but left unresolved on the day, pending further investigation. Based on their knowledge and instinct, specialists have made firm pronouncements but require more time to establish these as certainties. In some cases, where subsequent research has proved the specialist right, items have been followed up on a later *Roadshow*.

The first *Roadshow* in the 1986 season was filmed in May at Barnstaple's North Devon Leisure Centre. While walking past a long queue on the way to his table, Peter Nahum noticed a large painting held between two pieces of cardboard. Two hours later, this painting finally reached him and he was able to look properly at what turned out to be one of the *Roadshow*'s greatest finds. A specialist in nineteenth-century painting, Peter was one of the few people who would have known that he was looking at a long-lost work by Richard Dadd, which just goes to show that *Roadshow* finds can depend as much on luck as on knowledge.

## THE TRAVELLING PAINTER

Richard Dadd was born in Kent in 1817, the fourth of seven children. He began drawing at the age of thirteen, and at twenty he enrolled as a student at the Royal Academy Schools in London. Initially, he concentrated on subjects taken from history and literature, but his fame really grew in the early 1840s, when he began to exhibit paintings with fairy subjects – a popular theme in mid-Victorian Britain. In 1842, Dadd set off with his patron, Sir Thomas Phillips, on an extensive tour of Europe and the Middle East, including Belgium, Germany, Italy, Greece, Cyprus, Turkey, Syria, Palestine and Egypt. In November 1842, the party spent two weeks in the Holy Land, visiting Jerusalem, Jordan and the Dead Sea, a tour that included a crossing of the Engaddi mountains by night. It was during this trip that Dadd began to exhibit signs of the

madness that was to affect him for the rest of his life. He believed that it was his duty to kill those, such as the Pope, who held religious views that differed from his own. Having fallen out with Phillips, he returned to Britain. Such was his mental deterioration that he believed himself under the influence of the Egyptian god Osiris and, in August 1843, he murdered his own father. He fled to France, was captured, brought back to Britain and committed to Bethlem Hospital in London. He remained there until 1864 when he was transferred to Broadmoor, where he died in 1886. At Bethlem, Dadd was encouraged to paint, and sometimes he used his notebooks and sketchbooks to produce works documenting his tour with Phillips.

Peter Nahum, who had seen many examples of Dadd's work during his career as an auctioneer and art dealer, believed that the large watercolour shown to him in Barnstaple was one of a series painted by Dadd at Bethlem in about 1845. Having had it for years, the owners had hung it in their living room but, believing it to be a print, were about to put it away in the garden shed when they brought it to the *Roadshow*. Though certain of his attribution, which was also based on the French inscription on the back of the painting, Peter knew he could not prove it without further research, and so he filmed it without a valuation.

Encouraged by the BBC, Peter set to work. Archives at the Bethlem Royal Hospital Museum revealed that the painting could be one of three watercolours known to have been painted there but subsequently lost, while further evidence was supplied by a sketchbook in the Victoria

& Albert Museum. In 1857, three Dadd watercolours owned by the Preston collector Thomas Birchall were loaned to the Manchester Art Treasures Exhibition. One of these was entitled *Halt in the Desert*. Also known as *Encampment* or *Moonlight in the Desert*, this appeared to be the painting discovered in Barnstaple. In 1862, the same painting was shown at the International Exhibition in London, where a critic described it as having '*a wild feeling, one hardly knows whether more poetical or insane...*' At that point this painting, and the other two – catalogued as *Dead Camel* and *Moonlight in the Desert* – disappeared, perhaps lost when Thomas Birchall's collection was dispersed.

## A PROVENANCE CONFIRMED

With the attribution confirmed, the painting, now with its full title, *The Artist's Halt in the Desert*, appeared again on a *Roadshow* in 1987, and Peter was able to provide many details about the painting and its history. He established that among the group around the camp fire are Sir Thomas Phillips and Dadd himself, seated on the far right. The same year, the painting was acquired by the British Museum via a private treaty sale arranged with the owners, for a price of £100,000. This included a contribution from the National Heritage Memorial Fund. At the time, it was the most expensive item to have been found on the *Antiques Roadshow*.

Since then the painting, now acknowledged as a major work by Dadd, has been widely exhibited in the UK and abroad, and has also been included in exhibitions in Mexico, the United States and Abu Dhabi.

# AN ALBUM
# OF FILIPINO
# WATERCOLOURS

During its long life, the *Roadshow* has made a number of overseas programmes, including several in Europe. Sweden, France, the Netherlands, Gibraltar, Ireland and Malta have all hosted the programme, but it was in Belgium that the *Roadshow* made one of its biggest and most valuable finds. In February 1995, the team visited the Salle de la Madeleine in Brussels, and it was here that a Belgian couple brought in an album containing twenty-five watercolours depicting life in and around Manila in the late nineteenth century.

The owner's story was that the album had been commissioned from the artist, José Honorato Lozano by his great-great-grandfather, a tobacco merchant, so that his family, and particularly his children, would have a record of their time in the Filipino capital. As he looked through the album's colourful, highly detailed and often entertaining images Peter Nahum, the paintings specialist on duty, described it as, '*a kind of pictorial diary that today transports us to another world*'.

Though little known outside the Philippines at the time, Lozano was an important local artist who specialised in this kind of topographical material. Born the son of a lighthouse keeper in about 1820, by the age of thirty or so he was regarded in his own country as a watercolourist without rival. He was particularly associated with the local *costumbrista* tradition, namely the painting of local views as souvenirs for foreign visitors to Manila. He died in 1885, and so this album was probably produced towards the end of his life.

The owners clearly revered it as a memory of their family's nineteenth century history in Manila, but they were astonished when Peter Nahum valued it for £100,000, at the time one of the highest valuations in the *Roadshow*'s history. '*I am flabbergasted!*' was the shocked response.

At the time, some thought that Peter had been over-generous in his valuation of a set of watercolours of limited interest by a painter hitherto unknown in Europe. However, when the album sold later at Christie's, it fetched over £300,000. Although extraordinary at the time, this was reinforced by a further Christie's sale, in October 2015, when eleven similar views by Lozano, entitled *Types and Costumes of the Philippines*, sold for £266,500.

# PAUL STORR SALTS

*'They were the most beautiful sculptural objects and made by one of our greatest-ever silversmiths.'*

Brand Inglis

A curious fact of *Roadshow* life is that some of its greatest finds only just make it onto the show. Typical is the story of the set of four Paul Storr salt cellars filmed at Salisbury Cathedral in 1990. The owner came to reception with one of the salts in a brown paper bag, thinking it was made of brass and wanting to know what it was. Penny Brittain, then working on reception, saw the Paul Storr mark and asked him if he had any more. When told there were three more, Penny begged him to go home and fetch them without, of course, revealing anything about them. The owner was reluctant but agreed when offered a taxi to take him home. He did not reappear for ages and everyone had almost given up hope. Finally, near the end of the show, he returned with his wife and all four salts and was filmed by expert Brand Inglis as the last item of the day.

## SILVERSMITH TO ROYALTY

Paul Storr (1771–1844) is generally considered to be the most important of the silver and goldsmiths working in Britain during the Regency period. He registered his mark at Goldsmiths' Hall in 1792, having served a seven-year apprenticeship with the influential, London-based silversmith Andrew Fogelberg, and during the next thirty years developed his reputation as the most creative silversmith of his time. He worked initially on his own and later with the famous firm of Rundell & Bridge. In 1805, the company became Rundell, Bridge & Rundell, and included among its clients some of the wealthiest and most influential people in Britain, including George III, the Prince Regent, and their consorts. Storr designed and made many of these prestigious pieces. He become a partner in the business in 1811 but left ten years later to start his own business in partnership with John Mortimer, continuing to design and make fine things until his retirement in 1839.

Paul Storr's fame as a silversmith is based on his exceptional technical virtuosity, his attention to detail and finish and his creative imagination. It is widely believed that none of his contemporaries could match his particular skills.

The four silver gilt salts were modelled as shells supported by mermaids and mermen. Three carried marks for 1813 and one for 1811, along with the maker's mark for Paul Storr. During the filming, Brand Inglis suggested that the inspiration for the fluid, revived Rococo design may

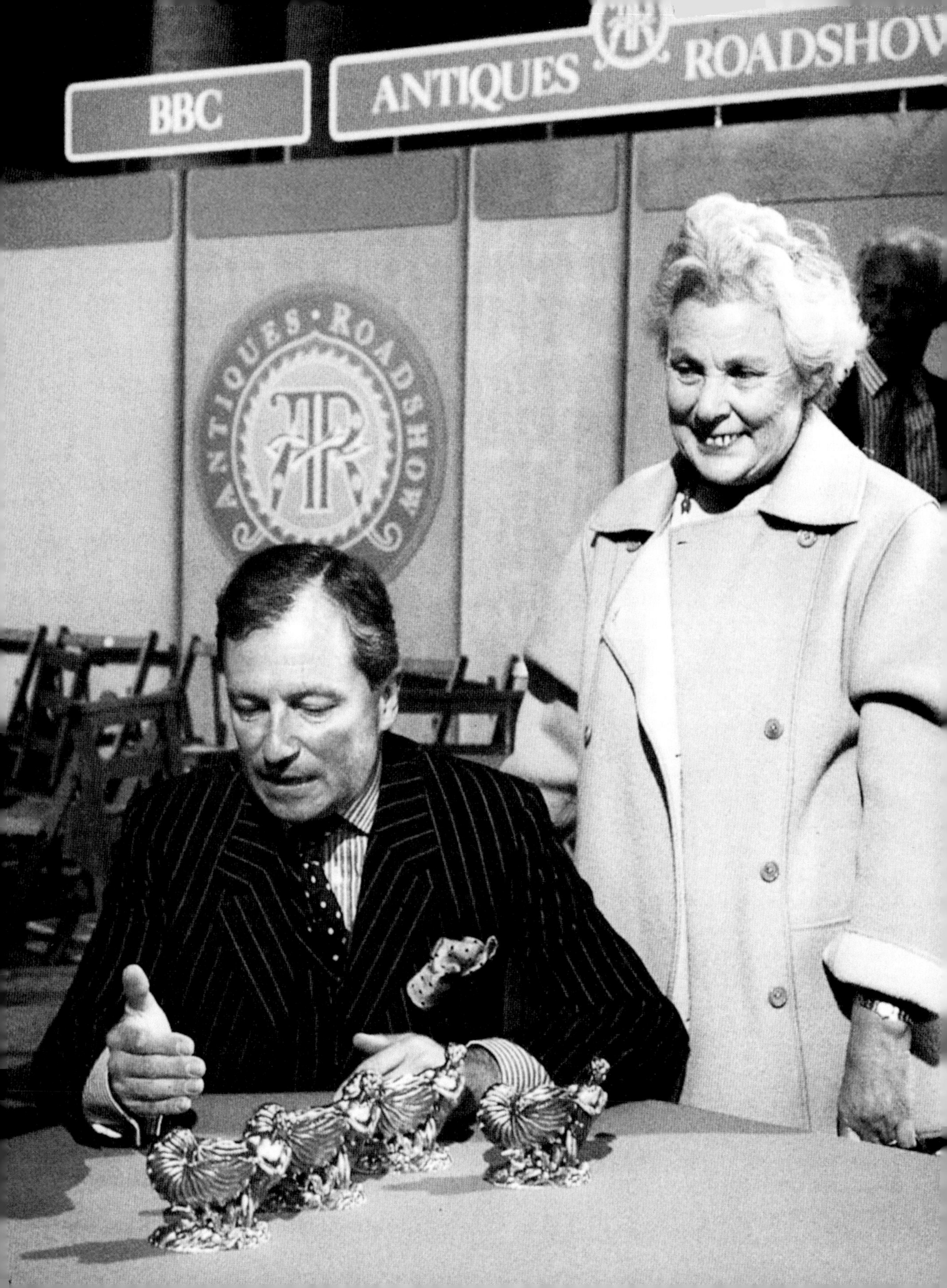
BBC
ANTIQUES
ROADSHOW
ANTIQUES · ROADSHOW

have come from an eighteenth-century piece by the silversmith Nicholas Sprimont (later the founder of the Chelsea porcelain factory) in the Royal Collection at Windsor Castle. He felt that, as Storr was frequently working for the Royal family, he could have had ample opportunity to see and admire pieces in the Royal Collection at Windsor. The Regency period in Britain was famous, not only for the extravagant lifestyle of the monarchy and those associated with it, but also for inventive and elaborate styles of design, particularly in the decorative arts. There were many influences, including earlier styles such as Gothic, Rococo and Classical, along with a taste for the exotic, the latter notably underlined by the famous Royal Pavilion in Brighton. At the same time, there was a dawning awareness of the importance of the Renaissance, with the salts also reflecting the styles associated with artists such as Cellini. There is a set of three similar salts in the collection of the Virginia Museum of Fine Arts in the United States, perhaps based on a design by the English sculptor William Theed.

## A MUCH UNDERRATED TREASURE

The owner, a quiet man clearly surprised by the whole filming process and the excitement generated by the salts, knew little about them. He had not considered them to be of any value, and said that his parents, who had been in service, had been given the set as a retirement present. His father had passed them on to him before his death six years ago, and since then they had lived in a plastic bag at the bottom of a bedroom cupboard. His response to Brand's valuation of £40,000 was to say: '*If my daughter-in-law hadn't told me the* Roadshow *was coming to Salisbury, the salts would still be sitting at the bottom of that cupboard. If anything had happened to my wife and I, the children would have had no idea of their value. They would probably have gone in a job lot house clearance.*'

Later, the salts were sold at auction for £66,000 to the Salters' Company and are now in Salters' Hall in the City of London.

# A RENAISSANCE GOLD PLAQUE

Objects of high quality and value made before the seventeenth century have always been *Roadshow* rarities, mainly because they have been well known, appreciated and documented for centuries. Also, relatively few of importance remain in private hands. There was, therefore, great excitement in Farnham's Sports Centre, in 1991, when a lady brought in a magnificently modelled gold plaque made in Italy between 1570 and 1580. Simon Bull, the *Roadshow*'s clock specialist on that day, was luckily on hand to share his great knowledge of Renaissance works of art with the owner.

Today the Renaissance, which started in Italy in the founteenth century, is universally acknowledged as a period of extraordinary creativity in the development of modern Western culture. All art forms – architecture, painting, sculpture, metalwork and jewellery, ceramics and glass, textiles, even arms and armour – were affected by a style that drew most of its inspiration from the Classical world, and its leading artists – Leonardo, Michelangelo, Cellini and so on – have long been household names. Also important were the great dynastic families of Italy, the Medici and the Borghese, who competed to have the finest things from the greatest artists and craftsmen of their time.

Pierced and set with cornelians, the solid gold plaque is modelled in relief with a scene depicting Atalanta hunting the great boar that had laid waste the lands of King Oineus, sent as a punishment for his failure to give thanks to Artemis after a successful harvest. At the heart of the lively scene, Atalanta has just fired the arrow that will bring down the boar. This classical Greek legend was popular with Renaissance artists.

Simon knew the legend and, more importantly, he knew of similar gold plaques in a museum in Berlin. He suggested that together they formed a set of six, originally intended to be mounted on a magnificent ebony cabinet made for the Borghese family. At some point, the cabinet had been lost or destroyed, but the plaques had survived, despite being made of gold. At one time the plaques were attributed to Cellini, but Simon knew that this was not now the case, though he was unable to identify the actual maker.

The owner knew little, except that it had been bought by her father in a sale at a time when such wonderful things were still accessible to a collector. Valued at £50,000 in 1991, this Renaissance gold plaque would now fetch at least ten times that, or even very much more.

# A DELFTWARE
# TURK'S HEAD

*'I know nothing about it — it just lives on the mantelpiece. It isn't even insured.'*

When the *Roadshow* visited Birmingham in 2000, the highlight of the day turned out to be a small pottery head and shoulders model of a Turk wearing a turban. Crudely modelled and brightly coloured, it seemed at first sight to be only of limited interest. However, John Sandon knew better, recognising it at once as an extremely unusual example of early English Delftware.

Delft is a widely used term to describe earthenware covered with an opaque, white, tin glaze and then freehand painted in blue and other colours. Also known as faience and maiolica, this type of pottery was made in many countries from the Middle Ages to the nineteenth century. Spain, Italy, France, Germany and Holland were the main centres of production, with the term Delft, or Delftware, reflecting the Dutch origins of many of the styles, shapes and designs. The inspiration was mostly Far Eastern, with the white-glazed pottery being a crude attempt at imitating the look of white Chinese porcelain. At the same time, the Middle East was also important, with many styles echoing the period of Islamic domination in southern Europe.

## AN EXTREMELY RARE EXAMPLE

Dutch and Italian potters probably brought the technique to Britain in the seventeenth century and, for a while, blue and white and polychrome Delftware was the most significant type of pottery made in Britain between the 1650s and the early eighteenth century. It was then replaced by the much improved white earthenwares and creamwares developed in Staffordshire from the 1730s. There were a number of Delftware production centres, although the main ones were in London, Liverpool and Bristol. Most potters produced functional domestic pottery, plates, dishes, bowls, mugs and tiles, with blue being the dominant colour. However, ceremonial chargers and punchbowls were also made, some with complex polychrome decoration that sometimes echoed Chinese styles and others with royal portraits or biblical scenes.

The young lady owner who had brought in the Turk figure knew nothing about it, other than that her aunt had lived in the same house since the 1920s, and had always had it on the mantelpiece until she died, aged 94. When the owner inherited it, she had thought nothing of it but had kept it because her aunt had liked it.

John Sandon then told her about English Delftware, and identified the Turk's head model as an extremely rare and early example, probably dating from the late seventeenth century. Although tin-glazed figure models were not unusual in Italy, France or Holland, very few were made by British potters. A number were recorded, including figures of Charles I and Apollo, along with a curious comic character called No-Body, from a play called *No-Body and Some-Body*, published in 1606. Also popular were cats, both seated and lying down, with a version of the seated cat serving as a jug. John explained that the Turk's head was particularly unusual and, though it had a maker's mark on the base, he was not able to identify it.

## A FAMILIAR MOTIF

The Turk's head is a familiar decorative motif in British history, with its origins probably linked to the Crusades. All over Britain, and particularly in sea ports, there are pubs called *The Turk's Head*. There is also a knot called a Turk's Head, and decorative pottery and porcelain featuring Turkish-style figures was popular throughout the eighteenth and nineteenth centuries. This

Delftware Turk's head was probably inspired by a European model, and thus may have been made by a potter with European connections. Despite some chips and minor damage – not unusual with Delftware – John was confident that the Delftware Turk's head would fetch £50,000.

Sometime later, the Turk's head appeared in a ceramics sale at the auctioneers Phillips in London, but failed to sell. It was then sold privately to an American collector, via a leading London dealer who specialised in early English pottery, for a sum roughly equivalent to John's *Roadshow* valuation. At the time, it was one of the most important examples of early English pottery to have been discovered by the *Roadshow*.

# A PAIR OF REGENCY
# PEAT BUCKETS

An unexpected find at the Whitchurch Leisure Centre in 2001 concerned a pair of massive peat buckets, made in Dublin at the start of the nineteenth century. Christopher Payne was delighted to be able to examine the buckets and discuss them with the owners, because eighteenth and early nineteenth century Irish furniture is rarely seen on the *Roadshow*, especially in England. He explained, '*Peat buckets weren't made in England, Scotland or Wales and so these are rare and highly desirable. I love the swirling ribbing that goes all the way down the bucket; this is exceptional as the usual decoration is parallel ribbing. The brass bands show that they were made the same way as barrels. They are also the largest peat buckets I have ever seen.*'

As Irish woodlands were steadily depleted from the sixteenth century onwards, the peat bogs became the primary source of fuel for both homes and industry. The gathering of peat turf was, therefore, necessary at all levels of society, although landowners generally had the right to cut the peat. Buckets such as these would have stood either side of the main fireplace in a grand house, topped up by the servants from peat stores in the outhouses.

These buckets had a lovely patina, the result of having been in the same family since they were made, and thus in regular use for decades. In their way, they were classic examples of Irish furniture, with distinctive details and styling that set them apart from English furniture of the Georgian period.

Christopher pointed out that their poor condition was part of their appeal. '*They have been heavily used for nearly 200 years and, frankly, they were falling apart. One was held together with binder twine and the brass bands were loose. They needed a bit of work and a good polish but they were far more appealing and valuable in that condition than if they had been heavily restored.*' For this reason, he valued the pair at £50,000, a price that would be difficult to sustain today because of fluctuations in the Irish market.

# A WILLIAM ORPEN
# PORTRAIT

*'What started out as a copy became a major Orpen discovery, and revealed a First World War mystery – the*
Roadshow *at its best.'*

Rupert Maas

In 2009 the *Roadshow* returned to Greenwich, a classic Thames-side setting framed by glorious architecture. The sun shone and people turned out in their thousands. It was a typically diverse day, with several items inevitably linked to the river and its history.

A gentleman brought in a striking portrait of a beautiful girl, which he believed to be a copy of a painting by William Orpen. At first sight, expert Rupert Maas agreed with him, but then began to have doubts. Before too long, Rupert realised that he wasn't looking at a copy, but probably at an original painting by Orpen. The situation was further confused by Orpen having signed the painting in a coded way.

## THE WAR ARTIST

Sir William Orpen was the most successful British artist of the early twentieth century and the most famous portrait painter of his age. Extravagant, outgoing and a lover of the high life in all its forms, Orpen was also a great painter with a distinctive style that combined modernism with a healthy respect for Vermeer, Velásquez and other European masters. During the First World War, he was appointed an official war artist, given the honorary rank of major and sent to France in the spring of 1917. He began with portraits – of Sir Douglas Haig and others – and then widened his brief to include battlefield scenes creating, in the process, some of the greatest works produced by the war artists' scheme.

The owner knew little about the painting but liked it very much and, encouraged by Rupert, he warmed to the idea that it might actually be by Orpen. However, with the limited research facilities available to him at the *Roadshow*, Rupert was not able to confirm the Orpen attribution, so he valued it for £20,000 to £30,000, pending further research. In due course, Rupert established that the portrait was indeed by Orpen and also that it was a second, hitherto unknown, version of a famous painting in the Imperial War Museum. At that point he revalued it for £250,000.

In the winter of 1917, William Orpen met and fell in love with a young Belgian girl named Yvonne Aubicq, who was to occupy a major place in his life, and his heart, until 1928. He

*After the filming the second version of Yvonne's portrait was briefly reunited with the Imperial War Museum's famous original, on the left.*

immediately painted her in the direct and provocative manner for which he was famous, planning to show this portrait of Yvonne in an exhibition to be held at Agnew's in London, early in 1918. He then remembered that, as an employed official war artist, he was only allowed to paint war pictures or those with war themes. In addition, the contract issued to official war artists stated that all paintings completed while 'on duty' were to be offered to the government, which had first refusal, and had to be submitted for censorship. As a result, no private work could be undertaken. To overcome this difficulty, he titled the painting *The Refugee*. He then went even further down a dangerous route by renaming it *The Spy*, and inventing and widely distributing a story about a glamorous German spy named Frida Nater, captured and shot by the French, whom he had been able to paint shortly before her execution.

## A GLAMOROUS STORY

According to Orpen's story, Frida was granted a last wish – to wear clothes of her choice for her execution. She chose a magnificent fur coat and, when the order was given, she dropped the coat and faced the firing squad completely naked, perhaps in the hope that the soldiers would not be able to carry out their orders. Nevertheless, she was shot. Inevitably, the truth came out, and Orpen ended up in trouble with the War Office. However, he recovered from this setback and continued to work as a war artist, not only throughout the duration of the war but also at the Paris Peace Conference in 1919. Now called *The Refugee* once more, this portrait of Yvonne is among over 130 works by Sir William Orpen in the collections of the Imperial War Museum.

Once all this had been established, the owner decided to sell the painting. At first, it was going to be sold at auction, and then it was sold privately, and is now in a private collection in Australia. The price paid was in the area of Rupert's revised valuation.

# A CHURCHILL CIGAR

Sometimes objects are brought to the *Roadshow* and, although they do not have any significant financial value, they offer an unusual and often personal insight into great moments in history. Inevitably, many of these tell stories about global conflict in the twentieth century. A typical example occurred at Lincoln Cathedral in 2009, when a man brought in the stub of a cigar purportedly smoked by Winston Churchill.

Throughout the Second World War, a series of international conferences was held by the leaders of the Allied countries to determine strategy, to plan future action within the various theatres of conflict and to plan the postwar peace. There were over twenty people involved, some of whom are household names, intricately and enduringly associated with the shaping of the modern world, while others languish in obscurity, remembered only by specialist historians. One of the most important conferences was held in Casablanca, North Africa, in January 1943. Churchill (the British prime minister), President Roosevelt of the United States and General De Gaulle of France were present, along with teams of military and civilian advisors. Among the decisions made were the declaration of the doctrine of unconditional surrender, the invasion of Sicily to take place later in 1943, the commitment to an invasion of mainland Europe in 1944, the ongoing support of Russia, greater support from Britain for the Pacific war and the creation of a Free French force under de Gaulle.

The owner of the cigar stub revealed to Fiona Bruce that, while serving in the British Army, his grandfather was employed as a butler during the ten days of the Casablanca conference. At some point, he had collected one of Churchill's cigar stubs, along with place markers bearing the names of important people attending the conference, including Harold Macmillan (later a British prime minister), Lord Alexander and King Peter of Yugoslavia.

Churchill, famously, was a great cigar smoker and around the world there are many cigar stubs and, indeed, whole cigars associated with him. Fiona pointed out that the provenance was all-important, as it is with all objects connected to famous people. The owner replied that he only knew what his grandfather had told him, and saw no reason to doubt his word. Given that the Churchill connection seemed definite, and the historical location important, the cigar stub was valued at £600–£800.

VIEIL ANVERS · OUD ANTWERPEN

# A STEIFF TITANIC
# BEAR

*'I got such a shock. I just couldn't believe it. I just rocked backwards and forwards. It's better than the stock market.'*

This was the reaction of a Melbourne lady who had just heard that her teddy bear was worth $200,000. In 2005, the *Roadshow* visited Australia, with two locations, Sydney and Melbourne. The first programme was filmed at Sydney University, the second in Melbourne's great exhibition building, a remarkable legacy of the International Exhibition of 1880, and the oldest building of its kind in the world still in regular use as an exhibition centre. Both shows had a ticketed attendance of 2,000, and both days produced some extraordinary and unexpected items, many of which were only indirectly connected to Australia's history. Among the most exciting was this black teddy bear. The catastrophic loss of the RMS *Titanic* on 15 April 1912 was commemorated in many ways, but one of the more unusual was the decision by the German toy maker, Steiff, to produce a black, grieving teddy bear as a memorial to those who had lost their lives, especially children. A small number were made, perhaps around 600 in different sizes, and the bears were distinguished by their black mohair fur and red-rimmed eyes, the latter to underline the grief affecting people around the world after the loss of the ship. It might have been more logical for Steiff to have produced a white polar bear toy, but it was believed at the time that a black, grieving bear would have greater appeal, and be more directly sympathetic to the disaster and its global impact.

## TEDDY BEAR FEVER

Steiff, a Stuttgart company set up by Margarete Steiff, in 1880, was well known internationally as the maker of the world's first jointed plush bears, invented by Margarete's nephew Richard in 1902 and introduced at the Leipzig Toy Fair in 1903. Hitherto, most animal models and toys had been presented on four legs, but Richard's breakthrough was to design a bear that stood up on its hind legs. In 1907, Steiff sold over 970,000 bears and teddy bear fever had gripped the world. By 1912 the teddy bear, named after the US President Theodore (Teddy) Roosevelt, had become one of the world's most popular toys, with manufacturers in many countries following Steiff's lead. However, Steiff had carefully developed and maintained its reputation as the maker of the best bears, underlined by the famous metal button label to be found on the bear's ear, which had been introduced in 1904.

Early Steiff bears can be valuable, with the best examples fetching £100,000 or more, but everything is dependent upon the condition. Most bears have, understandably, been much played with, often by more than one generation of children in a family, and so very few have survived in anything that might resemble their original, mint condition. It is not known how many *Titanic* bears were sold or how the public, and children, responded to a toy with so sad a story. It seems likely that the few survivors in good condition may have spent much of their lives at the back of cupboards or the bottom of trunks, forgotten from one generation to the next.

The *Titanic* bear shown at Melbourne was the first to be seen on the *Roadshow*. Others had appeared on the market – in 1990 a bear in excellent condition had sold at Christie's in London for £91,000. This gave expert Hilary Kay a benchmark figure for the Melbourne bear, which was brought in by a teddy bear and doll enthusiast who had first seen the bear some years before when she sent one of her bears to a restorer. When the work had been done, the restorer had sent her a photograph of her bear seated beside a black *Titanic* bear, something she had heard about but never seen. A year later, the restorer had called her to ask if she was interested in buying the black bear. Realising that she would probably never get another chance, and that it might be the only one in Australia, she agreed to buy it for $40,000. So, when she came to the *Roadshow*, she really wanted to find out whether she had paid the right price, and hoped that it might now be worth $60,000.

When the owner had recovered from her shock at hearing the $200,000 valuation, Hilary asked her if the bear had a name.

'*Oh no*,' she replied, '*I hadn't called him anything, he just sat on top of the cupboard.*'

In 2012, to mark the centenary of the disaster, Steiff reissued the *Titanic* bear in a limited edition.

# A WATERLOO CHEST

A small wooden cupboard, surmounted by a carved recumbent lion, was an unexpected find when the *Roadshow* visited Poole in 1998. Roy Butler, the militaria specialist on duty that day, knew exactly what it was. *'It was a great day for me. I'd heard about Waterloo chests and seen photographs of three, but I'd never seen and handled a real one until the owner brought this one to me.'*

The Battle of Waterloo in 1815 was an event of crucial importance. It saw the final defeat of Napoleon, ending twenty-three years of war between Britain and France, and also made possible the shaping of modern Europe. In a famously long and hard-fought battle, the French army was overcome by a coalition of British, Dutch, Belgian and Prussian armies under the command of the Duke of Wellington. The outcome was, as Wellington famously remarked, '*a close run thing*'.

Soon, the battlefield, and the buildings and other features on it, became a site of pilgrimage, attracting visitors from many countries. Booths were set up to sell souvenirs and relics from the conflict. A large elm tree, under which Wellington sheltered while his armies were readying for battle, was a particularly popular spot, and visitors flocked there to touch the tree and take away pieces of it. Soon, so much bark had been stripped off by souvenir hunters that the tree began to die. In 1818, an enterprising Englishman called John Children bought the tree from the Belgian farmer in whose field it was growing. From its timber, a throne was made for George IV as well as a number of chests and other, smaller souvenirs. Roy Butler explained that all the chests seemed to be similar, with two doors set with laurel wreaths and the lion on top representing the Lion Mound on the battlefield, above the word *Waterloo*.

The owner had acquired the chest from her father who had owned it for years and never liked it. Not realising its significance, he had been about to consign it to the coalshed when she had rescued it. It had been restored and she began to research its history. She discovered the connection with the Battle of Waterloo but, with no idea of the cupboard's rarity and importance, was very surprised when Roy valued it for £25,000.

# THE CREDENZA
# STORY

One of the challenges facing *Roadshow* experts is the need to be aware of changes in fashion, taste and patterns in collecting, and the resulting fluctuation in values caused by these changes. Values quoted ten, twenty or thirty years ago, while accurate at the time, may now be significantly different, and they can have gone up and down.

The area most affected by these changes is furniture, and there have been major drops in the values of most eighteenth and nineteenth century pieces. One of the most important examples of nineteenth century furniture to be seen on the *Roadshow* appeared at Wisley in 2003. This was a magnificent credenza, or dining room sideboard – one of the best pieces of Victorian furniture that John Bly had ever seen. He pointed out the lavish style and decoration, made from over twenty different types of wood, and with details in ivory, and said that such a piece was a triumph of the cabinet maker's art and was either a special commission or was made for one the great international exhibitions.

The owner said it had been given to her as a wedding present about ten years before by a great aunt who had emigrated to South Africa, leaving the credenza in storage for twenty or thirty years. She said, '*It just arrived on the doorstep well after our wedding, I had no idea what I was getting.*'

John explained that the key thing about important furniture, particularly of the nineteenth century, was the identity of the designer or maker. He went on, '*This was a period when design and craftsmanship were all-important, a time when traditional skills were being augmented by the intelligent use of machinery. There was also a demand among the newly wealthy industrialists and others for the best, and this is the best.*'

The owner had been able to establish that the original owners were the Baird family from Kelso in Scotland, and their initials inlaid on the front of the credenza matched the initials on the still-surviving gateway to their former house. George Alexander Baird was a famous amateur jockey, race horse owner and breeder whose family wealth came from iron and coal, and he would have been the ideal owner for such an extravagant and opulent piece of furniture.

John's valuation highlighted the importance of identifying the designer or maker. '*If we can trace it to a maker, it's worth in excess of £100,000. If we can't, then I'm afraid it's only worth £50,000.*' At this point the owner nearly fainted. Today, the valuation would be lower for this credenza, which while magnificent, is still anonymous, and so this is a classic reflection of changing tastes and fashions in the marketplace.

# A FRANCIS SOUZA
# PAINTING

*'This painting by Souza hangs on the bedroom wall, so I have been sleeping beneath it for most of the past ten years. Certainly, if the place burns down, it was always going to be the thing I'd rescue first.'*

One of the *Roadshow*'s more unusual London locations was the Dulwich College Picture Gallery, visited in 2008. Most of the filming was done in the garden, but several items were filmed inside the gallery, a sometimes daunting experience for specialists who found themselves in the shadow of a Rembrandt or a Gainsborough. Nevertheless, some interesting and unusual paintings appeared, not least one by the Indian artist, Francis Newton Souza, generally known as F. N. Souza.

Born in Goa in 1924, Souza was brought up as a Catholic and educated at St Xavier's College, Mumbai. Later, he attended an art school there but was expelled for supporting Indian independence. In 1947, he joined the Communist party and, the same year, was one of six founder members of the Bombay Progressive Artists' Group, which introduced Indian artists to international, avant-garde movements, such as Cubism and Expressionism, while retaining an awareness of India's own art history. It was set up a few months after the 1947 Partition of India and Pakistan, an event seen by the group's members as an impetus to create a new and contemporary art style for a modern India still dominated by conservative and traditional ideas and styles. Their aim was to paint with a new sense of freedom relating to content and technique, while acknowledging universal laws concerning aesthetics and colour composition. The group had largely dispersed by 1956, but its influence lived on, helping to shape the nature of modern art in India and, more importantly, giving it an international standing.

## AN EXPERIMENTAL ARTIST

In 1948 Souza held his first exhibition in London, moving to Britain the following year. Other exhibitions followed and, by 1955, his reputation was established. His style, according to the critic John Berger, was an eclectic mixture of Expressionism, Art Brut and British Neo-Romanticism, often overlaid with eroticism. An experimental painter throughout his long career, and an artist who pursued his own particular sense of beauty in the human body (which he saw as wild, noble, fragile and corruptible), Souza was one of the first Indian artists whose work was widely appreciated

in Europe and the United States. In 1967 he moved to New York, receiving the Guggenheim International Award and staying there until he returned to his native India shortly before his death in 2002. His obituary in the *Times of India* stated: '*With a few slashing lines and a raw, expressive energy, Francis Newton Souza stripped away all subterfuge… the seamy side of life or the steamy, he laid it bare.*' He holds a unique place in the pantheon of India's most important modern painters.

In 2010, a sale at Christie's of paintings and drawings from Souza's estate raised over £5 million. His work is exhibited in the Tate Gallery, and in major collections in India, Europe, the USA and Australia. In 2015, a major work by Souza sold in New York for $4 million, establishing a new world record for an Indian painting and a reflection of Souza's global importance.

Rupert Maas was very excited when he saw the painting – he recognised it at once as Souza's work – but was surprised and delighted that such an unusual work should come to a *Roadshow*. The owner's partner had bought it for £200 about ten years ago and it had been hung in his bedroom. Obviously attached to it, the owner said it would be the first thing he would rescue if the house caught fire. He knew about Souza, but was still surprised when Rupert valued it between £40,000 and £60,000. In 2008, the painting was sold at auction in New York for $75,000.

# MUGHAL BRACELETS

Over the years, many items brought to the *Roadshow* have offered rare insights into the great days of the British Empire, especially objects from India. From the eighteenth century onwards, many British families spent their lives working and living in India, as merchants, diplomats, civil servants and in the military, and when they returned to Britain they often brought with them treasures acquired during their period of service.

In 1995, an unexpected example was brought to John Benjamin, at Peebles, in the shape of a pair of richly enamelled gold bracelets dating from the middle of the nineteenth century. The family story was that the owner's great-grandparents had lived in India while her great-grandfather worked as a civil engineer. As was often the case, the family had come into contact with one of the local Indian princes, and the bracelets had been a gift from the prince to her great-grandmother.

This type of bracelet, worn on the ankle or upper arm, was traditionally associated with a wedding and could have been part of a bride's dowry. In this case, they took the form of confronting serpents, made from twenty-two carat gold, enriched with patterns of birds and flowers in red and blue enamel and studded with table-cut diamonds. Such jewels are associated with the Mughal period in Indian history.

Founded in 1526, the Mughal dynasty came to dominate many parts of India and had a long-lasting impact upon art, architecture, design and decoration until it ended with the death of Emperor Bahadur Shah in 1858. Jewellery was particularly important, with the wealth and status of both men and women reflected in the amount of extravagant jewels worn all over the body. In styles that bring together Mughal craftsmanship and Middle Eastern decoration, the jewels feature gold and silver metalwork in complex patterns, enriched with colourful enamelling and inset with diamonds and other gems. Mughal jewellery was designed to decorate the whole body, from the turban to the toe, and so the range included turban pins and ornaments, hair-pieces, ear-rings, nose rings, necklaces, bracelets, finger and toe rings, hand ornaments, amulets, belts, hip chains and much else besides. The actual weight of jewels worn and displayed underlined the wearer's status. The great diversity of surviving Mughal jewellery reveals both its importance and the huge number of workshops that must have been kept busy making it all over several hundred years.

In 1995, John Benjamin valued the bracelets for £10,000 to £15,000. Today, that price would probably have increased considerably, thanks to the great interest now shown by modern Indians in their history and culture.

# SCOTT EXPEDITION PHOTOGRAPHS

---

*'Had we lived I should have had a tale to tell of the hardihood, endurance and courage of my companions, which would have stirred the heart of every Englishman. These rough notes and our dead bodies must tell the tale.'*

Robert Falcon Scott

There is something extraordinarily powerful and emotive about objects that tell the story of polar exploration, and over the years the *Roadshow* has been fortunate to find items that bring such stories to life. Some of the most notable have been those associated with expeditions to Antarctica led by Captain Scott and Ernest Shackleton. Some were objects carried, worn or used by members of the expeditions, but better known and generally more accessible are photographs taken on the journeys to and from Antarctica and the South Pole. All the major expedition teams included photographers and their names are well known: Frank Hurley travelled with Shackleton and Herbert Ponting with Scott, and their remarkable images tell their stories with great clarity and timelessness.

## A GREAT ANTARCTIC EXPLORER

Robert Falcon Scott joined the Royal Navy in 1881, aged thirteen, and pursued a conventional, if unremarkable, naval career which was somewhat overshadowed by family and financial difficulties. In 1899, a chance meeting with Clements Markham, President of the Royal Geographical Society, resulted in Scott's appointment as leader of the British National Antarctic Expedition, better known as the Discovery expedition, after the name of the ship commanded by Scott. This sailed in August 1901, finally returning to Britain in 1904, after a challenging voyage during which great discoveries were made, although the expedition did not actually reach the South Pole. One major legacy of the voyage was the enduring rivalry between Scott and Shackleton, a member of the Discovery team. Back in Britain, Scott made the most of the expedition's achievements and the boost it had given to his career. In 1910 he was given command of the second British Antarctic Expedition, generally known as the Terra Nova expedition, again after the ship. After various setbacks, Scott and his chosen team finally set off for the South Pole in November 1911, in the full knowledge that the Roald Amundsen, the Norwegian explorer, was already ahead in the race to the Pole. The outcome is well known. When Scott reached the Pole on 17 January

1912, he found that Amundsen had beaten him by five weeks. He wrote in his diary: '*The worst has happened. All the day dreams must go. Great God, this is an awful place.*' During the long return journey from the Pole, Scott and his four companions died in March 1912, just eleven miles from a stores depot that would have saved them. Their bodies and all the records were finally recovered in November 1912.

## PICTURED AT THE BOTTOM OF THE WORLD

Also discovered was their camera, and with it what came to be one of the most famous of all exploration images. As Hugh Bett, the *Roadshow*'s book specialist, said when he found the photographs at Bolton in 1997: '*This is the most famous of all images, found undeveloped in the tent with the bodies. It was taken by Birdie Bowers, seated front left, and you can see by his hand the string*

*he pulled to release the camera's shutter.'* This extraordinary and evocative photograph shows the five members of the team at the South Pole and, although not composed by Herbert Ponting, it is always included among the many expedition photographs taken by him. As the expedition's official photographer, Ponting took over 1,700 glass plate negatives, including some early colour images. He also used an early movie camera to capture sequences of life in the Antarctic camps. After the expedition's disastrous end, Ponting's photographs became a kind of memorial to Scott and his team, and were widely published. On his return to England, there was an exhibition of the photographs, and portfolios of some of the best images were published.

## SAVED FROM DEMOLITION

The owners of the photographs, who worked in housing development, revealed that over a weekend they were clearing the garden of a large house due to be demolished. *'We were considering taking some of the plants before the bulldozers moved in and we saw what looked like the back of a large picture frame leaning against a wall. When we picked it up, we found it was a portfolio with these photographs.'*

Hugh went on to explain that, although the Ponting polar photographs were well known and existed in considerable numbers, the actual portfolios from that first exhibition were very rare and he had only ever seen one complete set before. These were not in the best condition, but the portfolio with the images was still worth £5,000. Today, that portfolio would be worth considerably more.

# THE BLUE JOHN
# STORY

Those working on the *Roadshow* often expect to come across items with a particular relevance to the location, for example a local type of pottery or porcelain, or a piece of furniture in a regional style. That this does not always happen can be explained by the fact that many things made locally were not necessarily sold locally. For example, Staffordshire potters could not stay in business if their products were only sold in Staffordshire.

However, there are plenty of occasions when this rule did not apply. When the *Roadshow* visited Buxton's Pavilion in 2001, on the local wish list of several of the show's specialists was a good piece of Derbyshire Blue John. This semi-precious mineral, a form of fluorite, is associated with just a few mines in the Castleton area of Derbyshire and, since it was first discovered, only fifteen Blue John veins have been identified, each with its own distinctive colouring and patterning. It is famous for its banded colouring in tones of blue, purple and yellow, which may explain the origin of the name, from the French *bleu-jaune*. Exploited commercially since the early eighteenth century, polished Blue John has been used in panels to decorate fireplaces, turned on lathes to form chalices, bowls, obelisks and other decorative shapes and also set into jewellery. Manufacturer Matthew Boulton often used the mineral in conjunction with ormulu and gilded silver for his neo-classical vases and candlesticks. In the nineteenth century, the production of Blue John ornaments was greatly increased to provide souvenirs for the expanding Derbyshire tourist trade. Nowadays, most of the deposits are nearly exhausted, with just a couple of mines still in use, so production is generally small scale. However, the discovery of a major new Blue John vein in 2013 may mean that large items could be made once again. The production process is complex and time-consuming, as the raw mineral coming out of the ground is fragile and easily crumbled. To make it stable, it must be left in the open air for a year, then heated with a resin (originally pine but now epoxy) to drive out air pockets and make it strong enough to be sawn, turned on a lathe and polished.

On that day in Buxton in 2001, a visitor brought in some magnificent examples of Blue John, including a tall standing cup and cover, along with samples of the mineral to explain the production process. Several *Roadshow* specialists were very pleased to have their dreams realised by the sight of such splendid examples. With good eighteenth century examples of Blue John fetching up to £10,000, it was not difficult to put a £2,000 to £3,000 valuation on the cup and cover that appeared at Buxton.

# QUEEN ANNE'S TRAVELLING CHEST

*'It's always been known in the family as the Queen Anne chest. I have no idea where it genuinely is, or isn't, but I have known it all my life.'*

Looking at furniture has always been part of the *Roadshow* experience, and throughout its long life some exceptional and valuable pieces have been discovered and discussed. The range of pieces seen has been comprehensive, from early medieval to late twentieth century. In Cirencester, John Bly described a metal-bound chest as the earliest piece of furniture he had ever seen while, at the other extreme, Paul Atterbury talked about a 1960s plastic pod chair. Throughout the *Roadshow's* early years, high-quality antique furniture was extensively featured. More recently there has been a shift in emphasis – fewer pieces are being brought to the *Roadshow* and those are largely late Victorian or from the twentieth century. This is a reflection of both the changing nature and age of the audience, together with a universal, dramatic and wide-ranging loss of interest in traditional antique furniture. As a result, it is increasingly unusual to see important examples of pre-nineteenth century furniture on a typical *Roadshow* day.

## TOO GOOD TO BE TRUE?

The exception to this occurred in 2012 at Cawdor Castle when a lady brought in a small, extravagantly made and richly decorated travelling chest of drawers that seemed to date from the start of the eighteenth century. Emblazoned on the top were the initials 'AR', possibly for Anne Regina. The chest provoked immediate and extensive discussions between Christopher Payne and other *Roadshow* specialists. The old antiques adage – that if something looks too good to be true then it is too good to be true – encouraged some to believe that it was a late nineteenth or early twentieth century copy, made at a time when such pieces were at the height of their popularity and antique dealers sometimes put aside their scruples. Others took it at face value, as a remarkable survivor from about 1705. Christopher Payne spent a long time considering it, noting the details and quality of its manufacture, and its exceptional original condition, including the silk lining in the drawers. By the time he filmed it, Christopher had decided that the chest was genuine, but he acknowledged that without further research he could not say if it had actually come from the royal household or whether it had actually been made for Queen Anne, as the initials on the top suggested.

The owner knew little about it, other than that it had been acquired by two spinster great-aunts in the 1880s, remaining in the family ever since. She did not know whether it was genuine or not, but an earlier valuation of around £600 had led her to doubt its authenticity. She was clearly surprised when Christopher told her that he believed it to be genuine, and even more so when he valued it at £20,000 to £30,000. He explained that this provisional valuation would be significantly increased if subsequent research could establish a definite connection to Queen Anne. After the *Roadshow*, the chest was shown to curators at the Victoria & Albert Museum, who declared it to be genuine and expressed an interest in acquiring it for their collections. It was subsequently taken to Hampton Court, where it was again declared to be genuine. Careful and thorough research seemed to link the chest to the Royal household, and suggested that it may even have spent time in the Palace. Like the V&A, Hampton Court expressed an interest in acquiring the chest.

## AN EPIC JOURNEY

For a while the chest fulfilled its original purpose, travelling around Britain, across the Atlantic to New York and covering far more miles than it could ever have done while in royal service at the start of the eighteenth century. It appeared at major antique shows and, in the end, was sold privately. The final price was not disclosed, but the owner said that in the end the sum realised was a great deal more than Christopher Payne's original *Roadshow* valuation.

There is no doubt that this chest was an exceptional and highly unusual piece of eighteenth century furniture, and one of the great *Roadshow* discoveries. It is, perhaps, a pity that it was lost to the national collections but its journey underlined the point that, in today's market, exceptional furniture can be priceless while the honest, but unremarkable, pieces that were popular thirty years ago are now almost unsaleable. That could also explain why so little furniture makes its way onto the *Roadshow* today.

# BUFFALO BILL'S GLOVES

Objects associated with famous people are always *Roadshow* favourites although, as the specialists frequently point out, provenance is everything.

In 2006, the programme visited Holkham Hall in Norfolk. Among the treasures brought in that day was a pair of gloves belonging to Buffalo Bill. William Frederick Cody, popularly known as Buffalo Bill, was a scout, rancher, hunter, soldier and showman whose life spanned an extraordinary chapter in the history of the United States. He was a larger than life character with a reputation that often crossed the boundaries between fact and legend. He is best known today as a showman. In 1883 he launched Buffalo Bill's Wild West, a circus and touring show that was to occupy him for much of his life. This immense undertaking, involving hundreds of people, animals, cowboys and native North American demonstrations and historical recreations, brought his particular vision of American cowboy life to thousands as it travelled across North America. In 1887 Cody brought the show to Britain, as part of the celebrations for Queen Victoria's Golden Jubilee, visiting London, Birmingham and Manchester, where it stayed for a few months, proving to be as popular here as it had been in the United States. Two years later, the show toured Europe. The vision of cowboy life presented in the show is said to have established that particular idea of American history, and was particularly influential when Hollywood began to exploit the story of the cowboy.

An important part of the show involved the sale of souvenirs, many of which survive today. However, few can be directly connected to Buffalo Bill himself. The leather gloves that appeared at Holkham, with their decoration in Sioux or Pawnee style, did have that connection. The owner's grandfather had apparently been keen on animals and had his own private zoo. While the Wild West show was in Britain, he went to see it, met Buffalo Bill and bought some animals from him for his zoo. According to the family story, he acquired the gloves during that visit, either by buying them from, or being given them by, Buffalo Bill. The gloves are typical of those worn by Cody during his show. Inevitably, many pairs of gloves associated with Buffalo Bill are known, but this pair was exceptional, thanks to their condition and the provenance leading back to Buffalo Bill himself. For this reason, Hilary Kay valued them at £10,000. The delighted owner has kept the gloves, treasuring them as an important part of her family history.

LEFT PAGE: *top left, the late Dominic Winter; top right, Elaine Binning; centre, Lee Young; bottom left, Rupert Powell; bottom right, Susan Rumfitt.* RIGHT PAGE: *top left, Wayne Colquhoun; top right, Alastair Chandler; centre, Lawrence Hendra; bottom left, Cristian Beadman; bottom right, Chris Yeo.*

# AN ALMA-TADEMA PORTRAIT

'*The news of the discovery of this important lost work has stunned the art world. This is one of the best pictures we have ever seen on the* Roadshow *in its entire history. Alma-Tadema is the most valuable Victorian artist today.*'

Rupert Maas

During the *Roadshow*'s long life, swings in taste, and hence in value, have affected many areas of art and antiques, and the programme's specialists have had to adjust their views accordingly. During the late 1970s, British Victorian paintings were still riding the boom that had started in the mid-1960s. Since then, the market has been a bit of a roller coaster, with prices falling during the last years of the twentieth century. In the last twenty years there has been a recovery but, as in so many fields, this has tended to apply only to the best items.

## VICTORIAN SUPERSTARS

In the late nineteenth century, certain British artists enjoyed levels of popularity and wealth that are almost inconceivable today. Painters like Millais, Leighton and Alma-Tadema were household names, their fame reaching far beyond the boundaries of the art world. Frederick Leighton was knighted, then made a baronet and his funeral in St Paul's cathedral, on 8 February 1896, drew crowds of thousands and made the front page of the *Illustrated London News*. Another great name was Sir Lawrence Alma-Tadema. Born 'Lourens' in the Netherlands in 1836, he lived in Europe until 1870 when he moved to London, making the city his home for the rest of his life. His reputation, already established in Europe, expanded massively after the move to England, greatly helped by his development of a distinctive style that drew inspiration from civilisations of the past, notably the Roman Empire. His paintings blended historical research, extravagant decoration and eroticism in a memorable way, and were extremely popular. In 1873, he and his wife were given a kind of British citizenship at the behest of Queen Victoria; then, in 1879 he was made a full Royal Academician; in 1882 his first major retrospective exhibition was held; and in 1899 he was knighted. Financially astute, Alma-Tadema became a wealthy man, with paintings regularly selling for sums between £2,000 and £6,000. Alma-Tadema's fame and wealth were based on his long-standing ability to give the public what it liked, namely richly detailed and historically accurate depictions of beautiful people in classical settings.

After his death in 1912, Alma-Tadema's reputation steadily diminished to the point where his work had become virtually unsaleable by the 1950s. A major painting, *The Finding of Moses*, that had sold for over £5,000 in 1904, was sold for only £265 in 1942 and failed to sell at all in 1960. The same painting sold in 1995 in New York for £1.75 million, and again in 2010 for $35 million, at the time a record for a Victorian painting.

In a period when modern painting enjoyed great popularity, there was a ready market for printed reproductions of famous works and, unlike many of his contemporaries, Alma-Tadema was famous for controlling the rights to his paintings and the income derived from their sales. Many of his major works were issued as engravings and he was careful to control not only the finances but also the quality, particularly as many of the editions were signed by him. He was able to do this because, throughout his life in Britain, Alma-Tadema worked closely with one engraver and etcher, his friend Léopold Lowenstam, who had moved to Britain around the same time, in 1870. What was not known until the *Roadshow* visited Arley Hall in 2016, was that Alma-Tadema had painted a portrait of his friend Leopold.

## A TOKEN OF FRIENDSHIP

Painted in 1883 as a wedding present for Léopold and his wife Alice, the painting was brought to the *Roadshow* by Léopold's great-great-grandson. It had been shown at the Royal Academy in 1884 and at an exhibition in Liverpool in 1913, but since then had never left the family, and so was unknown to Rupert and other Alma-Tadema specialists. It is a very personal portrait, clearly a token of friendship, and shows Léopold at work on a copper plate, preparing a print from the painting set up in front of him. As Rupert said at the time: '*There are hardly any portraits of engravers at work, and this is one of the most telling and the most beautiful.*' The owner confirmed that Léopold and Alma-Tadema were close friends, and that his great-great-grandmother had been a governess for Alma-Tadema's children.

Rupert valued the painting at £200,000 to £300,000 – a vast sum for a *Roadshow* painting, but well below the millions that a great Alma-Tadema classical scene would now fetch. He explained: '*This doesn't quite reach that because it isn't a classical subject and it's not large. But it is very, very good and shows another more painterly side of his work than the more typical girls in togas sitting on marble benches.*'

Since the *Roadshow*, the painting has been on show in the Netherlands, Vienna and London, celebrating its discovery and its return to the Alma-Tadema catalogue.

# A COLD-PAINTED BRONZE PARROT

Models of animals and birds in brightly coloured bronze make regular appearances on the *Roadshow*. They tend to be products of a famous craft industry that is particularly associated with Vienna in the latter part of the nineteenth and the early years of the twentieth centuries. Few of these make it to the screen, but the parrot that appeared at the 1997 *Roadshow* at Newport, on the Isle of Wight, certainly did, mainly because of the model's exceptional size. It was this that first caught Eric Knowles' eye when he saw the bird across the crowded Medina Hall, as he explained: '*I have seen plenty of smaller birds, but never a life-size macaw like this. He looks as if he might fly off across the hall at any minute.*'

Eric immediately identified the maker as Franz Bergman, the owner of the most important of the many factories producing similar-coloured bronzes in Vienna at the time. The technique that made these models so distinctive was the process of cold painting, whereby bronzes cast from moulds in the factory are painted in great detail in life-like colours, often by women working at home. The colours, not fired on after painting, chip and flake easily, and so it is quite rare to find examples that are still in a good, original condition. Few of the sculptors are documented but the models, usually of all kinds of birds and animals, and often in small sizes, were hugely popular in Austria and throughout Europe. Human models were also made, including a range of Arab figures, reflecting the contemporary enthusiasm for orientalism and Middle Eastern styles, along with some tastefully erotic and often-hidden female figures. It is generally accepted that Bergman made the best cold-painted bronzes, and many carry his mark, either his name or a symbol with his initial. For his erotic range he used the name Namgreb (Bergman spelt backwards). However, over fifty factories in and around Vienna are known to have made cold-painted bronzes. Bergman himself died in 1936, his factory having closed in 1930.

Eric valued the macaw at £4,000, saying to the owners: '*I'm glad to see this handsome bird has enjoyed a caring home. The colours are still strong and fresh, which adds to the bird's value and rarity.*'

# VAN DYCK PORTRAIT

*'I bought it partly because I liked the frame and there was something about his ruffle and something about him telling a story — he looks quite an angry character.'*

It is quite rare for an important Old Master painting to be brought to the *Roadshow*, but that all changed at Newstead Abbey in Nottinghamshire, in 2012, when a local priest brought in a painting he had bought for £400 some years before from a Norwich antique shop. He talked first to Fiona Bruce who, having recently worked on a *Fake or Fortune* programme about Van Dyck, thought that the portrait had some Van Dyck-like details that should be checked. He said that he had bought it because he liked the frame and was intrigued by the character of the man depicted in the portrait. He explained that it had hung for a long time in the Retreat House that he ran, at one time falling off the wall and breaking his CD player. He knew it carried a label saying 'Sir A. Van Dyck', but had always assumed it to be a copy. Thanks to Fiona's enthusiasm the owner was asked to bring the painting to another *Roadshow*, held at the Royal Agricultural University in Cirencester. There he met Philip Mould who, by the end of the day, was convinced that he might be looking at a genuine Van Dyck. He asked the owner if he was prepared to submit the painting to a long process of restoration and analysis, something that Philip called the equivalent of an archaeological excavation, and the owner agreed to do so. This was the start of a long journey of discovery. During several weeks of work, all the later overpainting was removed, turning what had seemed to be a completed portrait into an unfinished sketch.

## INTERNATIONAL PORTRAIT PAINTER

Flemish-born Sir Anthony Van Dyck became the leading Court painter in Britain during the first half of the seventeenth century. Despite his early death in 1641, he set the style and the standard for English portrait painting for the next 150 years. Trained by Rubens, who called him his best pupil, he first came to Britain in 1620, where he immediately entered court circles. He then moved to Italy for six years, developing a highly personal style marked by the influence of Titian and Veronese. In 1632, he returned to London, partly at the instigation of Charles I, whose great enthusiasm for painting had led him to bring several European artists to his court. By July 1632, Van Dyck had been given a knighthood and the title of Court Painter to the King.

*Fully restored, and the attribution now certain, the Van Dyck portrait takes its place in the artist's catalogue raisonneé.*

Van Dyck enjoyed an immediate success, painting over thirty portraits of Charles I and many of other members of the royal family and the court. He developed his distinctive portrait style, which combined a relaxed elegance with a sense of authority. As the political climate in Britain worsened, Van Dyck spent time in Europe. Following a long illness, he returned to London in 1641, dying there in December.

Despite his short life, Van Dyck's output was prodigious, and inevitably much of his work has been lost. So, the possibility of the *Roadshow*'s discovery turning out to be a hitherto unknown Van Dyck was exciting. When the restoration process had been completed, the painting, in its new guise as an unfinished sketch, was shown to Van Dyck experts, and was accepted as genuine. Philip Mould, who had masterminded the painting's restoration, said: '*The painting's emergence from beneath layers of paint was dramatic. It's been revealed as a thrilling example of Van Dyck's skills of direct observation that made him so great a portrait painter.*' The owner was equally delighted and said that he hoped to sell the painting to pay for a new set of bells for his church to mark the centenary of the start of the First World War.

## AN IDENTITY CONFIRMED

As well as being accepted as a Van Dyck, the painting's subject had also been identified. In 1634, Van Dyck completed a large group portrait entitled *Magistrates of Brussels*. This painting was destroyed in 1685, but a grisaille sketch survives in Paris which reveals the composition. Van Dyck prepared a series of oil portrait sketches for all the sitters, three of which are known to have survived and by comparison with these, and another similar sketch in the Royal Collection, Philip was able to establish that the *Roadshow* portrait depicted another member of the group, shown on the far right in the grisaille sketch. Thus, a £400 anonymous portrait of an unknown man in a seventeenth-century style, bought partly because of the frame, turned into a sketch by Van Dyck of a magistrate of Brussels, now valued at £400,000. It is one of the *Roadshow*'s greatest finds, and illustrates the point that, on the day, expertise and instinct can only go so far, particularly with works of art.

# A STUART TABLE CASKET

The restoration of the monarchy in 1660 was widely celebrated throughout Britain, with many families able to express in public their relief at the ending of Cromwell's Commonwealth. This was expressed in many ways — more colourful and decorative styles of dress, commemorative pottery, notably Delftware portrait chargers and engraved drinking glasses. These appear on the *Roadshow* from time to time but much more striking, and much rarer, are caskets covered with colourful, and often symbolic embroidery, in various styles and techniques, including stumpwork. Very few of these survive in good condition as, in most cases, the colours have faded and the embroidery has been damaged by time and wear and tear. These embroidery-covered caskets and boxes were part of a general enthusiasm at the time for decorative needlework, and this included the making (to a very high standard) of bed covers, hangings, cushions and samplers, generally by the women and children of the household.

When an excellent example appeared at the *Roadshow* in Cheltenham, in 1995, it caused a great stir. Almost breathless with excitement, Victoria Leatham described how ladies in Britain's wealthy households would make embroidered panels using silks in glorious colours, ribbons and laces and gold and silver threads, which were then attached to the wooden casket, in this case with drawers concealed behind doors and a domed top. The subjects, usually inspired by Biblical stories, scenes from country life such as hunting, animals, birds, insects and garden flowers, reflected the revival of the monarchy and the new freedoms it represented. Victoria explained that these were celebratory pieces: '*When new, the colours would have been quite brilliant and garish, the sort of thing we might actually consider quite vulgar today. The couple embroidered on the doors could depict Charles II and his Queen, or even the owners of the house where this was made, probably in the 1660s.*'

Caskets like this were used as portable desks, jewellery boxes and vanity cases. Some contained secret drawers or compartments, often linked to the concealment of love letters by ladies enjoying, in a wider sense, the new freedoms set in train by the Restoration. This casket had been inherited by the owner about ten years earlier, having always been a family piece. At the time it had been valued at £3,000. Impressed by the quality of the embroidery, the original condition and the relative brightness of the colours, Victoria gave it a much higher value, £15,000 to £25,000. The family later sold the casket at auction for £21,600.

# HENRY MOORE LETTERS

---

*'As we approached Bracon Ash there was one tree cut down, it was a wonderful piece of sculpture, one yard of it especially — which I'd like to cut out, place on a base to keep near me when I'm working, perhaps call it Fecundity, for at front it has two large swellings which burst through the large mass like the breasts of a huge primitive woman.'*

Henry Moore

The most exciting *Roadshow* discoveries are often those that offer unexpected insights into the lives of famous people. At Syon Park in 1999, Clive Farahar, a *Roadshow* book and manuscript specialist since 1985, had one of his most memorable moments when a lady brought him eighteen illustrated letters written to her mother by Henry Moore.

After serving in the First World War, Henry Moore became a student at Leeds School of Art, where he met Barbara Hepworth. In 1921, he won a scholarship to the Royal College of Art, and it was while he was in London that he explored collections of primitive and ethnographic art. At the same time, he began to be influenced by sculptors such as Brancusi, Gaudier-Brzeska and Epstein and, guided by the artist and sculptor Frank Dobson, he abandoned the classical approach to sculpture, teaching himself the technique of direct carving. In 1924, Moore was awarded a six-month travelling scholarship, which he spent mostly in Italy. Returning to London, he began to carve in the style for which he was soon to become well known, producing reclining figures that brought together the influences of Michelangelo and Pre-Columbian Mayan sculpture.

## A GREAT FRIENDSHIP

When Moore was at the Royal College, he became friendly in about 1922 or 1923 with fellow student Evelyn Kendall. The details and precise nature of the friendship are not known, but Moore wrote long letters to Evelyn, full of thoughts about his life and work, and richly illustrated with drawings. These were the letters that the lady, who turned out to be Evelyn's daughter, brought to the *Roadshow*. Moore was famously a great letter writer and so, while these are not obviously love letters, their content reveals at least a close friendship with a degree of intimacy. They seem to have been written during a college vacation while Moore was staying in Norfolk, as there are references to local villages such as Bracon Ash and Mulbarton. He talks about the countryside and the details of the landscape, as well as his hopes and expectations

about becoming a sculptor. He describes his routine: '*I get up about 9 — begin carving about 10 — carve for an hour then stretch my legs by getting a pear or two from the tree, then carry on till 12.30 — carve again till 4.*' He also writes that he loves talking about '*myself and sculpture in particular*'. More mundane are plans for Christmas and a description of a visit to the dentist. There are also indications of a degree of intimacy: '*I'm going to bed. I'm tired. I mark myself beforehand 5/10. Goodnight Evelyn.*' These words are written above a self-portrait surrounded by nudes, including reclining figures and a mother and child, with the comment: '*These are all the work I haven't done.*'

## EARLY INSPIRATIONS

Within the letters are passages, like the one quoted above, that reveal his attachment to nature, and the close connections he was building between apparently abstracted sculptural forms and the constant inspiration of the natural world, themes that Moore was to pursue for the rest of his life. The many drawings scattered through the letters underline this, sometimes reflecting his already developing taste for the primitive.

Clive was very excited by the letters, seeing the extraordinary insight they offered into both Henry Moore's private life and a crucial period in his development as a sculptor. They indicate that he was already forming ideas and ways of thinking about the profession of sculpture as a student in his early twenties and these were to guide him for the rest of his life. Clive told the owner of the letters that, although the exact details of her mother's friendship with Moore would probably never be known, they were certainly close. There are two sculptures that seem to be related to Evelyn, dating from 1923 and 1924, in the collection of the Henry Moore Foundation. One is a head, and the other a nude torso.

Clive valued the letters at £50,000. Later, they were sold by Sotheby's for around £30,000, the price perhaps affected by the discovery that the Henry Moore Foundation already had copies of the letters. In any case, the owner was happy. '*I wanted them to be accessible to researchers and historians and they were too valuable to have in the house — and it paid a year's university fees for my two children.*'

# A MÄRKLIN
# TINPLATE BIPLANE

In 1987, while putting together an exhibition to be held at Sotheby's for *Save the Children*, Hilary Kay visited Chatsworth House and found a tinplate biplane sitting on a shelf and generally considered to be of little interest. It was borrowed for the exhibition and subsequently looked at in a new light by the Duchess of Devonshire. When the *Roadshow* came to Chatsworth ten years later, Hilary found that the biplane now resided in the gold vaults.

When it was filmed for the *Roadshow*, Hilary explained that the biplane was among the rarest of the many toys produced by German toy maker Märklin, with only two examples known – the one from Chatsworth and another belonging to a Thai prince. After the programme was broadcast, the BBC received a letter from a lady who had been a housekeeper at the school attended by the young Duke of Devonshire. She explained that the Duke and the Thai prince had been best friends and imagined that they had both been given their biplanes as Christmas presents, having made their choice from an early Märklin catalogue.

Established in 1859, the Göppingen-based company at first produced dolls' house accessories. Märklin soon developed into one of the greatest names in the German tinplate toy industry, producing a high-quality range of trains, ships, cars, model steam engines, construction kits and other toy novelties that were all remarkable for their attention to detail. There were few aeroplanes in the catalogue and this biplane, which would have been very expensive at the time, was not known to exist until the Chatsworth example was discovered. Large and intricately constructed, with celluloid-covered wings, the biplane was modelled on a Wright Brothers Flyer of about 1906 and designed to fly along a wire.

While, strictly speaking, the biplane was not a *Roadshow* discovery, as Hilary already knew of its existence at Chatsworth, the decision was taken to film it for the programme because of its great rarity and remarkable original condition. That decision seemed entirely justified when Hilary valued the biplane for £100,000.

*Deborah, Duchess of Devonshire during the filming of the* Roadshow *at Chatsworth in 1997.*

# THE COTTINGLEY
# FAIRIES

*'My heart was gladdened when out here in far Australia I had your note and the three wonderful pictures which are confirmatory of our published results. When our fairies are admitted other psychic phenomena will find a more ready acceptance.'*

Sir Arthur Conan Doyle

The unpredictable nature of the *Roadshow* makes every day different, and that is part of the appeal for specialists who have worked with the show for many years. Knowing that anything could turn up is always exciting, and when it does it is always unexpected. Sharing a story on the *Roadshow* brings together many things, including a sense of discovery, family and social history and sometimes significant value but, best of all, is being able to touch moments of real historical importance.

In 2008, the *Roadshow* went to Belfast to make a programme in the rather challenging setting of the old drawing offices at the former Harland and Wolff shipyard. The *Titanic* seemed likely to be the day's historical link but, as ever, the *Roadshow* had a major surprise in store, in the shape of two ladies with an old camera and some photographs. To an astonished Paul Atterbury, they revealed themselves as daughter and grand-daughter of Frances Griffiths, one of the two young girls at the heart of the famous Cottingley Fairies saga.

## JUST A FAIRY STORY?

In 1917 nine-year-old Frances Griffiths, who had recently returned with her mother from South Africa, was staying in Cottingley, near Leeds, with her aunt and her sixteen-year-old daughter, Elsie. The girls often went to the stream at the bottom of the garden, saying they were visiting the fairies that lived there. To overcome the family's disbelief, they borrowed Elsie's father's camera and took a photograph of Frances with the fairies. Two months later, they took another, this time of Elsie with a fairy. For a while the story was generally considered a prank and remained in the family but, in 1919, Elsie's mother Polly took the photographs to a Theosophical meeting in Bradford. From this point the story, to use a modern term, went viral, catching the contemporary enthusiasm for theosophy, spiritualism and psychic phenomena. While many dismissed the story as a hoax, it gained massive credibility when Sir Arthur Conan Doyle became involved. He not only believed the story, but in 1920 set out to

prove it conclusively. He gave the girls two better cameras and told them to take more fairy photographs. Over the next few days three more were taken. Two were similar in style to the first pair – the girls with fairies looking like cut outs – while a third was very different, with more translucent fairies among the grass. The publication of the photographs provoked a massive public debate, with many people insisting that they had been faked while others supported Conan Doyle. Eventually, interest in the story diminished and Frances and Elsie

got on with their lives. Interest revived in the 1960s and 1970s, and the photographs were tested and analysed in various ways that exposed them for what they were. However, the girls stuck to their story until 1983, when they finally confessed to the hoax. They had used cut-out fairies based on drawings of dancers in a 1914 edition of *Princess Mary's Gift Book* and fixed to plants with hatpins for four of the photographs, but Frances continued to insist that the fifth photograph was genuine, even though Elsie had said it was also a fake. In a 1985 interview, both women said it had been a prank that had got out of control. Elsie's view was: '*Two village kids and a brilliant man like Conan Doyle — well, we could only keep quiet.*' Frances was a bit more perceptive: '*I never even thought of it as being a fraud — it was just Elsie and I having a bit of fun and I can't understand to this day why they were taken in — they wanted to be taken in.*'

On that day in Belfast, Paul could not believe his luck. '*I had been fascinated by the Cottingley fairies story for ages, particularly in the way it was bound up with the rise of spiritualism during and after the First World War. To have the chance now to talk about it with Frances' family and to handle the actual*

*photographs and one of the Conan Doyle cameras, well, it was almost too much. It was one of those rare* Roadshow *moments when I really felt that I was touching history.'*

## A GREAT, ACCIDENTAL HOAX

Paul also pointed out that today the photographs simply did not stand up to scrutiny, as the way they had been taken with cut-out fairy figures was very obvious. In the 1920s, other photographers had taken similar fairy photographs to prove they were fakes, but no one had wanted to listen. And so the story had rolled on, to take its place as one of the great, if accidental, hoaxes of the twentieth century. For this reason, Paul valued the camera and the photographs for £25,000.

Despite Frances's confession and the now obvious nature of the hoax, the two ladies continued to insist that the rather more mysterious fifth photograph was genuine. '*So,*' said Paul, '*You still believe in fairies?*' After a pause, they both replied, '*Yes, we believe in fairies*'.

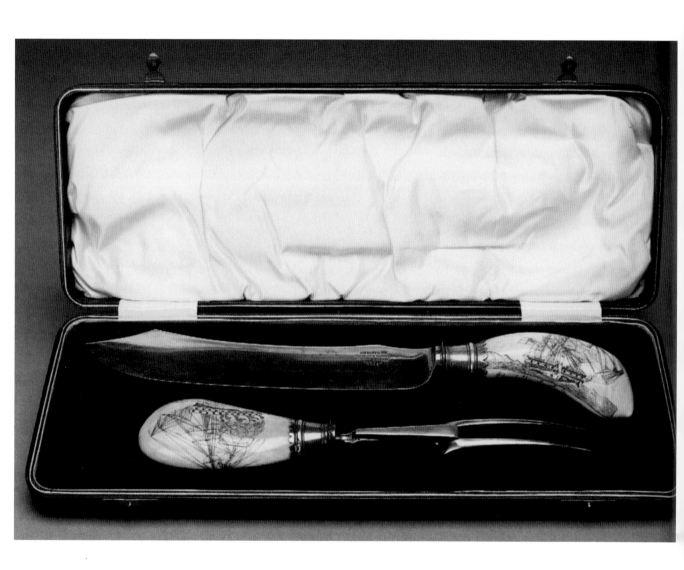

# SCRIMSHAW CARVERS

Scrimshaw, the collective name for decorative objects made by sailors – generally from waste materials associated with ships and the sea – makes regular appearances at *Roadshows*. Most common are the teeth and bones of whales engraved with scenes either of ship life or drawn from illustrated magazines, and made by sailors using hand-made tools. The long-established popularity of these has resulted in the widespread production of fakes and copies, and so definitive attribution of them on the programme can be challenging. Even rarer are those that can be attributed to a known engraver.

However, at a show in Scarborough in 2003, when faced with a boxed carving knife and fork whose handles were formed from engraved sperm whale teeth, Hilary Kay knew exactly what she was looking at. '*I saw the hand of Edward Burdett in the carving as soon as I examined the set,*' she explained. '*He has a distinctive style and was one of the earliest identifiable scrimshaw artists working in America.*'

Burdett, one of the best-known scrimshaw artists of his day, was born in Nantucket in 1805. A whaler all his life, he made his first whaling voyage aged seventeen on the ship *Foster*. One of the first artists to use the teeth of sperm whales, he quickly developed a characteristic and personal style of engraving. He died in a whaling accident aged just twenty-eight in 1833, when he was first mate on the whaler *Montano*.

The engravings on the carving knife and fork handles depict identifiable and documented scenes – a feature of the best examples of scrimshaw and important in establishing value. The fork handle shows the whaler *Daniel IV* on fire in 1828, fully laden with whale oil, while the knife handle depicts the *Elizabeth of London*, the ship that rescued the sailors from the burning *Daniel IV*. It is likely that the teeth were engraved at the time by Burdett, while the story was still fresh, and then mounted later on to the knife and fork.

Hilary valued the set at a conservative £10,000 to £15,000, knowing that it was likely to fetch much more if sold in the United States, the primary market for high-quality scrimshaw. In due course the family, who had owned the set since the late 1820s, decided to sell and, armed with the necessary CITES (Convention on International Trade in Endangered Species) certificate, they sent it to San Francisco, where it sold at auction for £33,000.

# NEWSPAPER POSTERS

*Roadshow* visitors are often very surprised to find that things that were worthless when produced have sometimes become valuable with the passage of time. This applies particularly to paper ephemera that was designed to be used and then thrown away. Newspapers are an obvious example, but old newspapers rarely have any value, as even those issued to mark an important event, such as a coronation or the outbreak of war, tend to be kept, and thus survive in large numbers. Far rarer are the posters with dramatic headlines issued on a daily basis to help sell the papers, for these were always thrown away to make room for the next day's poster on the stands.

There was therefore considerable excitement among the experts at Audley End in 2015 when a couple appeared clutching bundles of old newspaper posters. They told Clive Stewart-Lockhart that, when they bought the shop next door to the one they owned in Essex, they found a boarded up doorway connecting the two properties. They explained, '*When we took the boarding down, there were all these, just rolled up, scrunched up, wedged between two bits of wood, just over 100 old newspaper posters.*'

Clive went through them, pointing out that, while some were in good condition, others were in a dreadful state. However, more important was the story they told, for their time scale spanned the outbreak of the First World War and the early weeks of conflict. He pulled out one dated Wednesday 5 August 1914, with the headline: 'Britain and Germany at War', and then another, dated a few days earlier, which stated: 'Our Ultimatum to Germany'. He explained how, if put in date order, the posters would reveal the full story of the first few weeks of war, starting with the shock of the first casualties, and then the gradual build up as the war moved from being primarily a naval conflict towards the establishment of the British Expeditionary Force to be sent to Belgium and France. He highlighted headlines about German spies being shot, and Germans living in Britain being rounded up and said, '*These posters give us a remarkably direct view of history, enabling us to relive these events as they actually occurred, on a day to day basis. Their value as social history is probably more important than their financial value.*' Nevertheless, he put a value of £1,000 on the collection, knowing that there were many collectors keen on this kind of ephemera. The owner then revealed that he had offered them to the Imperial War Museum but they had decided they did not want them.

In many ways, this item represented the *Roadshow* at its best: a chance discovery of forgotten commonplace things that were not supposed to survive, and with really no value at all. Yet, a century on those same things had acquired, by the extraordinary and unexpected nature of their survival, both great rarity and historical and financial value.

# BEATRIX POTTER DRAWINGS

*'It was tremendously exciting and a wonderful find. It shows that Beatrix Potter did a lot of preparatory drawings, leading up to her famous characters. She worked hard at animals in human situations.'*

Clive Farahar

Over the years Beatrix Potter has made a number of *Roadshow* appearances, in one form or another. A signed first edition of *Peter Rabbit* and an early Peter Rabbit stuffed toy are among the finds that have kept the famous Lakeland author in the *Roadshow* spotlight, but these faded into insignificance when the programme came to Dumphries House in 2003 and a collection of twenty-three original drawings and watercolours by Potter appeared out of a case.

The appeal of Beatrix Potter is both enduring and international and the story of her life – from a comfortable London childhood to Lakeland farming and conservation – is well known. Born in 1866 and privately educated, she was drawn initially to natural sciences, and learned to draw as a botanical artist, specialising in the study of mycology. However, when she was unable to pursue this as a career, she began to write and illustrate children's stories for family and friends. She published her first book, *The Tale of Peter Rabbit*, herself in December 1901, in a black and white version that nonetheless established her style, and her way of integrating text and illustrations. A year later this little book was reissued by Frederick Warne, becoming an instant success, and marking the start of a publishing partnership that was to issue twenty-three Beatrix Potter animal books over the next few years.

## A FLAIR FOR MARKETING

A clever businesswoman, Potter exploited the marketing potential of her characters from the start, and so her familiar animals were soon decorating tea sets, board games, wallpaper and baby blankets. In 1905, using her book income and a small inheritance, she bought Hill Top Farm, near Sawrey in the Lake District, and this was to become her home for the rest of her life. She gradually extended her estate by buying adjacent properties, bred Herdwick sheep, fought hard to save the Lake District from development and, at her death in 1943, left her farm and estate, which then totalled over 4,000 acres, to the National Trust.

It is the illustrations that make Potter's books what they are. They spring from a long tradition of children's book illustration that developed in the late nineteenth century, thanks largely to new

colour printing processes. She knew that tradition well, having grown up with it, but developed it further with great sublety. She followed the fashionable enthusiasm for zoomorphism with animals engaged in human activities but her animals have a particular and distinctive charm that sets them apart. The detail is extraordinary despite the small scale, and the settings usually reflected the Lakeland landscape and the interiors of her house, Hill Top Farm.

The twenty-three drawings were brought in to the *Roadshow* by a man on behalf of his wife's family, who had farming connections with Beatrix Potter's brother Bertram. They had never been seen outside the family but their importance, as Clive quickly established, was that they predated the publication of *The Tale of Peter Rabbit*. Some carried dates in the 1890s, and the animals depicted, though in human clothes and situations, were distinct from the famous characters that she developed later. It is known that Potter used to make up illustrated stories for the children of family and friends, often written in exercise books with pasted-in illustrations, and these may have been drawn by her for such a purpose. For Clive, their importance was that they showed Potter experimenting with a style that she was soon to make her own. As he said: '*They show small animals like kittens or mice or rabbits in human settings doing human things. Some are sketches and some are half-finished, a kind of work in progress towards the Beatrix Potter we all know and love.*'

Today, with thousands visiting Hill Top Farm every year, and her stories and characters enjoying extraordinary popularity throughout the world, Beatrix Potter is a global phenomenon. Original drawings by her are rare, as most of those used in her books are either owned by the National Trust or are in museums and public collections around the world. There is a large collection of her letters and drawings in the Victoria & Albert Museum. Therefore, this collection of twenty-three drawings was both very rare and valuable. Clive valued some of the individual drawings at between £10,000 and £50,000, and had no hesitation is putting a price of £250,000 on the whole collection.

# 'THE WINNER' ENAMEL ADVERTISING SIGN

Traditionally, *Antiques Roadshow* is filmed on a Thursday, but in 2015 we opted for a family-friendly Sunday afternoon to stage an event at Walmer Castle, the Tudor fortress and picturesque home of the Duke of Wellington. Sure enough, the queues started gathering early. A lady at the head of the line, sporting a colourful T-shirt emblazoned with a large heart, typified the wonderful enthusiasm and good humour shown by all during this lovely sunny day on the Kent coast.

With no shortage of visitors, the potential for interesting finds was greatly increased. Miscellaneous specialist Lisa Lloyd was not disappointed when brought face-to-face with a rare, tinplate advertising sign. Made in the 1920s, this type of sign would have been a commonplace feature on our streets. Businesses and manufacturers jostled for space on buildings and hoardings, advertising every type of product imaginable on all-weather enamelled signs, emblazoned on sheets of milled steel. Many were later scrapped because of the wartime demand for metal, although plenty still survived. Appealing to an obvious section of the market, motoring-related signs can be particularly collectable and automobilia auctions are now big business. In addition, the sheer number of transport museums up and down the country is testament to the popularity of motoring nostalgia.

Lisa was in no doubt about the sign's rarity. Known as 'The Winner', this sign promoting BP petrol depicts a speeding, open-topped racing car, obviously powered by BP petrol, crossing the finishing line. It epitomises a golden age of early motoring but also speaks volumes about a post-First World War society, reeling in the wake of horrific events but also re-inventing itself amidst the hope and new ideals displayed in such exciting designs and graphics. The Art Deco period – which developed throughout the 1920s and 30s – is characterised by 'modern' ideals. This is manifested in many of the graphic renditions associated with flying, ocean liners, locomotives and cars, particularly racing cars. The art of conveying speed through interesting perspectives, angular and symmetrical slanting, graphic 'speed lines' and bold colours is much appreciated by collectors of such material. Add rarity to the mix and you have a classic recipe for a potentially valuable item. Well-known examples include the iconic 1930s poster by A.M. Cassandre (actually Adolphe Jean Marie-Mouron) of the French transatlantic liner *Normandie*, which frequently makes in excess of £10,000 at auction.

As is often the case, Lisa's excitement had to be kept in check so that nothing was given away, and the sign was readily scheduled for filming, along with its characterful owner! It helps to be cautious in such circumstances, though, as this sign has been cleverly copied, and several such fakes have appeared on the market over the last decade. The imitations are generally cold-painted, clever pastiches that utilise original metal signs – complete with rust – which, when over-painted, are then also aged. Lisa's careful inspection proved this sign's authenticity and she was confident that the chatty owner would be in for a surprise.

As the story unfolded on camera, he explained that while browsing through militaria in a shop twenty years earlier, he had

noticed the sign on the wall. He liked it and bought it for a mere £10. When pressed further, he revealed that the sign actually resided in his garage, intimating that his wife was not too keen on having it in the house. Nevertheless, he was happy to leave it there and admire it.

The owner's 'love' for the slightly rusty sign became obvious when, shortly afterwards, Lisa announced 'The Winner' as a highly sought rarity, valuing it at a staggering £10,000–15,000. At this point – in a state of shock – the gentleman leant over and, instead of kissing Lisa, kissed the sign! The audience was surprised too, and hearty applause ensured another classic *Roadshow* moment.

The owner still has the sign and, at the time of writing, has no plans to sell it. The record price achieved in 2005 for a version of this iconic advertising item was £28,000. For this *Antiques Roadshow* visitor, this really was a winner.

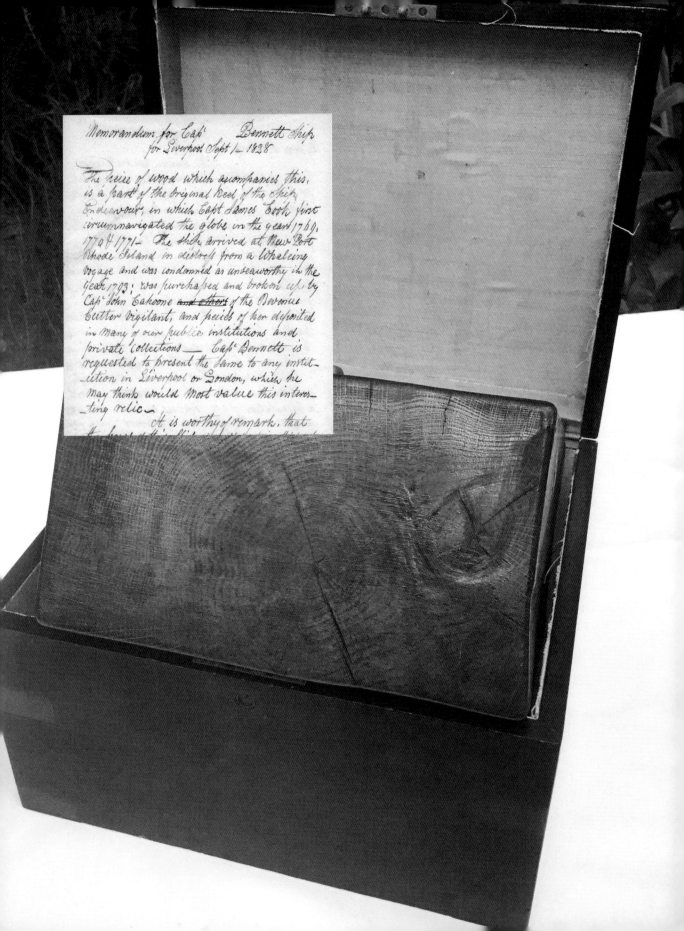

Memorandum for Cap.t Bennett Ship
for Liverpool Sept 1 — 1828

The peice of wood which accompanies this,
is a part of the original Keel of the Ship
Endeavour, in which Capt James Cook first
circumnavigated the globe in the years 1769,
1770 & 1771 — The Ship arrived at New Port
Rhode Island in distress from a Whaleing
Voyage and was condemned as unseaworthy in the
year 1793; was purchased and broken up by
Cap.t John Cahoone and others of the Revenue
Cutter Vigilant, and peices of her deposited
in many of our public institutions and
private Collections — Cap.t Bennett is
requested to present the Same to any instit-
-ution in Liverpool or London, which he
may think would most value this interes-
-ting relic —
          It is worthy of remark, that

# THE KEEL OF ENDEAVOUR

When the *Roadshow* went to make two programmes in Australia in 2005, no one quite knew what to expect. The small team of specialists from the BBC's programme was augmented by some locally recruited reinforcements whose knowledge of Australian history and culture proved to be invaluable. In the event, most of the major discoveries turned out to be British, but there were some significant Australian moments in both Sydney and Melbourne.

One of the most unexpected was a large, rectangular block of polished oak, claimed by the owner to be a section from the keel of Captain Cook's ship, *Endeavour*. As such, it represented a tangible link to the discovery of Australia by Cook in April 1770, and thus was a highly significant relic in the history of modern Australia. The immediate question was whether it was authentic. The owner, whose father had bought it in Boston, had undertaken extensive research in family and other documents and seemed able to take the story of the origin of the block of wood back to the early nineteenth century, and link it to the *Endeavour*. The key point was that wood from the *Endeavour* had been used in a series of later vessels, as was common at the time. He also believed that a larger section from the same keel was in a museum in Newport, Rhode Island, in the United States.

When Cook returned to Britain from his voyage in July 1771, he was received as a hero. His ship, however, was quickly forgotten. Immediately taken over by the navy, *Endeavour* was refitted as a transport ship and continued in naval service until 1775, when she was sold to a private owner. After some refitting, and with a new name, the *Lord Sandwich*, the former *Endeavour* came back into service as a transport ship for British troops during the American war of Independence. In 1778, she was in a group of ships sunk by the British to protect Saratoga harbour from the French fleet, and has remained there ever since. Various archaeological expeditions were launched to try to locate the wreck without success, until May 2016, when a team of archaeologists, backed by extensive documentary research and the most modern high-tech underwater mapping techniques, claimed to have identified the *Endeavour* among a group of thirteen sunken blockships. This may or may not affect the Australian claim, as the block of wood could have been removed during one of the *Endeavour*'s two refits, and kept by someone who knew its origin, or even rescued during earlier explorations of the sunken wreck.

At the time, this highly unusual story was discussed with the owner by Paul Atterbury, who remarked that a nominally worthless block of wood could be worth £100,000 as a vital part of modern Australian history.

# SUNBEAM-TALBOT 90 RALLY CAR

There is a story behind every item on *Antiques Roadshow*, but the best are often a blend of accidental discovery, classic endurance, dogged determination to see something important resurrected for future generations and a good splash of nostalgia and emotion, too. In 2010, the show did not disappoint when we set up in the glorious surroundings of one of Britain's largest parish churches – Beverley Minster. Situated in the beautiful East Riding of Yorkshire, the church is largely thirteenth century. However, such buildings bring with them the type of logistical problem that you might expect when making a television programme that attracts thousands of visitors; the appearance of an interesting car was obviously going to require some extra thought!

The vehicle in question – a gleaming, black Sunbeam-Talbot 90 – was parked on the Minster lawn and attracted a lot of attention prior to filming. Called a '90', simply because it could do 90 miles per hour, it transpired that the car once belonged to a farmer who had apparently used it to pull his pigs to market. He eventually left it in a barn from where it was subsequently rescued by the owner. Expert Jon Baddeley soon became aware of its real significance, signalled by the presence of a 'Rallye Monte-Carlo' plate affixed to the front bumper and dated 1953. Like most car companies, the incentive to enter cars competitively inspired Sunbeam-Talbot – part of the Rootes Group – to compete in famous rallies. Doing so both proved their vehicles and increased sales. Rallying was a huge spectator sport during this time. This car – it seemed – had a prestigious rallying history, driven by none other than the famous racing driver Stirling Moss and John Cooper, the editor of *Autocar*, with the navigator Desmond Scammell. Having won the Charles Ferro Trophy at the 1953 Monte Carlo Rally, the car also won the touring car class of the rally the same year and, until 1955, competed in several other prestigious rallies, including the Alpine, Tulip and RAC. Immaculately restored and shining brightly in the Yorkshire sunshine, the car fired up Jon's innate motoring interest. He happily eulogized over its racing pedigree and the importance of Stirling Moss's relationship to the vehicle, finally plumping for an unexpected £50,000 estimate – much to the wonder and surprise of the family. The daughters sat in the back seat of the car throughout the entire filming process.

However, the story has a slightly bitter-sweet ending: in 2016, the owner sadly passed away, leaving the family with a decision regarding the car. As it turned out, it was easily solved –

the eldest daughter decided to use the car at her wedding, even though she was heading for university at the time of writing, with no nuptial plans on the immediate horizon. However, the family feels that the car remains a fitting tribute to their husband and father and have no desire to part with it. Let us hope it fulfils that dream, in memory of a man who rescued a classic car and lovingly brought it back to life.

# CARPATHIA MEMORABILIA

The loss of the *Titanic* ranks, inevitably, as one the greatest maritime disasters ever, and over the years the *Roadshow* has seen its fair share of *Titanic*-related items. Some of these have told stories about other ships drawn into the disaster, such as the *Californian* and, more significantly, the RMS *Carpathia*. Built by Swan Hunter for Cunard, the *Carpathia*'s maiden voyage as a transatlantic liner was in 1903. On 15 April 1912, en route from New York to Fiume, she found herself near enough to the *Titanic* to pick up that ship's distress calls and, two hours after the *Titanic* had sunk, she reached the spot at 4am, having steamed at full speed through the dangerous ice fields, and was thus able to rescue 705 survivors from the lifeboats. Having picked up the last survivor at 9am, Captain Rostron then turned his ship round, and sailed for New York, where he docked on 18 April 1912.

*Carpathia*'s crew were all treated as heroes, and awarded special medals – made of bronze for the crew members and silver and gold for the officers. In addition, Captain Rostron was given a silver cup and awarded a knighthood. Later, President Taft invited him to the White House, where he received a Congressional Gold Medal. *Carpathia* returned to her usual transatlantic service and became a troopship during the First World War. She was sunk by a German submarine in July 1918.

In 1998, an extraordinary collection of *Carpathia* memorabilia was brought into the Poole *Roadshow* by an owner whose father, Dr Edward McGee, had been the *Carpathia*'s medical officer at the time of the tragedy, and so had been directly involved in looking after the *Titanic*'s survivors as they were brought on board. The collection included a photograph of Dr McGee, his gold *Carpathia* medal, a silver medal from the Royal Humane Society and a cigarette case inscribed: '*Presented to the Captain, officers and crew in recognition of heroic services.*'

Aware of the huge interest in *Titanic*-related material, and the importance of this particular group from one of the most senior of the *Carpathia*'s officers, Victoria Leatham valued the collection for £50,000.

# A LEICA II LUXUS CAMERA

*'The serial number was engrained in my head – 88840 – the holy grail of the camera world.'*

Marc Allum

The year was 2001. After making the short hop from its Bristol base across the Severn estuary, the *Roadshow* entourage set up shop in and around the recreation centre in Bridgend. Large queues were already forming, attracted by the excitement of the occasion and the great variety of items brought along, and it is no surprise that many of the *Roadshow*'s miscellaneous experts have their own favourite areas of interest, too. Specialist Marc Allum, for example, has always professed a keen interest in cameras and photographic history. Little did he suspect that a camera of immense rarity and value would find its way onto his busy table that very day.

## A SPECIAL MOMENT

As the affable visitor opened his bag and revealed by degrees – from a slightly worn crocodile case – a shabby-looking gold Leica camera, Marc recalls, *'it felt like a Holy Grail moment that was meant just for me'*. Experience counts for everything in these situations, but even specialists are apprehensive when confronted by an object of great rarity. Cameras are a particular minefield. Leicas, by the very nature of their collectability, have spawned many copies and Marc has seen his fair share over the years. On one occasion, he even filmed a counterfeit Leica II 1936 Olympic edition. Generally, fake cameras are rarely good enough to fool a specialist because the finishes – which try to emulate the Luxus model that Marc had sitting in front of him – tend to be lacquered polished brass rather than real gold plate. They are invariably based on mass-produced Russian copies of Leica cameras that were made in their millions. However, this particular camera, with its 88840 serial number, corresponded to a batch of four special edition 1932 Leica II Luxus cameras that are documented within the Leitz factory records.

At the time – and this is a measure of how the markets are both very liquid and, ultimately, subject to the vagaries of the world economy and emerging new collectors – Marc filmed the camera, estimating its value at several thousand pounds but commenting on the difficulty in pricing such rarities. The owner, himself a keen photographer, had been given the camera by a friend after the Second World War, but no real ownership provenance existed prior to this. He decided to keep the camera as an investment for his daughter. When the programme aired, the camera caused an explosion of interest. While enthusiasts debated its authenticity, it was featured in a mainstream camera magazine with quotes attributed to Marc that were never even made! Marc recounts how several collectors from as far afield as Japan contacted him in a bid to track down the camera, but he remained tight-lipped and the matter went no further.

## AN IMPORTANT LEGACY

The story could have ended there, but twelve years later the owner passed away, leaving the camera to his daughter, as promised, and she contacted the *Roadshow*. By this time, the market had changed considerably. With the emergence of a new collecting base, fuelled by the wealth of the Tiger economies of southeast Asia, the camera was exhibited in London and offered for sale at a specialist auction in Hong Kong. The fact that the whereabouts of the other three special editions remained unknown and a rare period advertisement showed that the crocodile skin case appeared to be the only one known, added to the speculation about what the camera might potentially make. The owner, who wished to use the proceeds to send her son to Harvard University in America, met Marc for a special surprise viewing of the Leica in London. Before the sale he was, once again, lucky enough to hold the camera, and this meeting was aired in a Christmas special.

There were many predictions – even extending up to a million pounds – as to what the camera might realise on the day, but when bidding finally stopped, the Leica had sold for a very healthy, premium-inclusive £479,156! This provided a happy ending to a *Roadshow* story that had spanned more than a decade. As far as we know, the lady's son made it to Harvard, too.

*Marc and the owner enjoy the Leica for the last time at a special London viewing before it was sold.*

# A TERRY FROST
# PORTRAIT

Paintings by modern British artists are rarely brought to the *Roadshow* but, when they do appear, there is always an interesting story. At Derby in 2014 a lady appeared with a portrait that seemed to have been painted on a section of a pillowcase. She explained to Philip Mould that it had been painted by Terry Frost when he was in a German prisoner of war camp.

When the Second World War broke out, Terry Frost joined the army, later transferring to the Commandos. Captured in Crete in June 1941, he then spent the next four years in various prisoner of war camps in Germany. In Stalag 383 he met the artist Adrian Heath, a fellow prisoner, who taught him to paint, as a way of overcoming the boredom and deprivations of camp life. The owner's father had been in the same camp at Hohenfels in Bavaria as Terry in 1943–44 and while he was there he had traded his pillowcase for a portrait, with Terry telling him that he was able to get four portraits out of each pillowcase. Much later, in the 1990s, the owner had met Terry Frost and he had told her later in a letter that he had painted about two hundred such portraits while he was a prisoner.

Back in Britain after the war, Terry Frost went to a number of art schools and worked as an assistant to Barbara Hepworth. At first, he continued to paint in a figurative style, but he quickly moved towards a more abstract approach. His first solo exhibition was held in St Ives in 1947 and this set him on his way to becoming one of Britain's leading abstract artists. For much of his life he lived in St Ives, and was closely associated with other Cornish-based painters, notably Roger Hilton, whom he had also met during the war. Frost became a Royal Academician in 1992 and was knighted in 1998.

Philip Mould was intrigued by so early an example of Frost's work, containing as it did little to suggest the route that Frost was later to take. However it clearly showed, along with the other portraits in the pillowcase series, the struggles of a painter learning his craft.

Since the *Roadshow*, the owner has given the portrait to the National Army Museum, along with the letter from Terry Frost and a diary belonging to her father.

# MARC BOLAN'S GIBSON 'FLYING V' GUITAR

*'I was so nervous I could hardly press the strings down!'*                    Marc Allum

*Antiques Roadshow*'s specialists include several musicians, such as guitarist Marc Allum. As you would expect, any specialist with a passion for playing the guitar is likely to have more than a passing interest in vintage instruments, particularly those associated with legendary musicians.

The *Roadshow* at Swansea Town Hall in 1999 had got off to a busy start. Marc was working his table when he noticed a couple with a guitar-shaped case in the queue. Guitar cases promise a great deal, but you never really know until you open them up. Nonetheless, by the time the owners reached his table, Marc's interest was already piqued.

## ONE OF THE GREATS

It was a heart-stopping moment for Marc when the case was opened, revealing a distinctive Gibson Flying V. This in itself is valuable enough, but the bridge of this particular instrument was engraved with the name 'Marc Bolan'. As most people know, Marc Bolan was a legendary British glam rocker of the 1970s. Born Mark Feld in 1947, Bolan's early career encompassed acting, modelling and music, but the formation of his band Tyrannosaurus Rex (later becoming T. Rex) in the late 1960s, set him firmly on the path to stardom. Songs such as 'Debora' (1968), 'Telegram Sam' (1972) and '20th Century Boy' (1973), were huge hits while Bolan's androgynous look paved the way for the likes of David Bowie. Bolan was also a successful poet – published in 1969, his book *The Warlock of Love* sold 40,000 copies and, despite its critics, proved to be one of the country's bestselling books of poetry.

After a brief discussion with the owners, Marc Allum established a sound provenance for the guitar. It was used by Bolan in many iconic publicity shots and on programmes such as *Top of the Pops*. This particular guitar had also come from the same batch as one made for the guitarist Jimi Hendrix. Flying Vs have always been rather flamboyant guitars and on stage Bolan had visually exploited its striking appeal.

The couple also had a gold lamé stage suit and a sailor suit, both worn by Bolan. The story went that they had become friendly with the person who ran the official Marc Bolan fan club and they could not resist the chance to own these items!

In front of the camera, Marc displayed a combination of nervous anticipation mixed with awe and he was so nervous that he could hardly press down the strings. Rarely, in musical terms, is it possible to connect with such an influential and iconic figure as Bolan, touching an instrument that actually belonged to him. The situation was made even more emotive, given Bolan's sad and untimely death in a car crash, at the age of twenty-nine. A Mini – driven by his girlfriend Gloria Jones – hit a tree and Bolan, who was not wearing a seatbelt, was killed instantly.

It was obvious that the husband and wife owners were staunch fans of Marc Bolan and T. Rex. Marc Allum enthused over the items before estimating the value of the guitar at £50,000–60,000, the gold lamé suit at £8,000–12,000 and the sailor suit at £8,000–12,000. In reality, the guitar later came to auction and realised a commission-inclusive £36,000, the lamé suit made £7,000 and the sailor suit was privately sold but later valued by Sotheby's at £14,000. This may have been a little short of the estimates, but what price can you place on the experience of owning and handling such incredible items?

'*I've got a Rolls-Royce 'cos it's good for my voice.*' Marc Bolan (1947–1977)

# GRAHAM SUTHERLAND PAINTING

Attic discoveries have their place in *Roadshow* history, but one of the most unusual of these came to light at Chartwell House in 2002, when a lady brought in a painting which she claimed was by Graham Sutherland.

When she was a child, her family had lived next door to Graham Sutherland and she remembered seeing him at work in his studio. She had always loved his house, a typical sixteenth century white-painted, weather-boarded house in the heart of the Weald of Kent and decided at an early age that one day it would be hers. Sutherland had lived in the house for nearly forty years and so was unlikely to move. However, after his death in 1980, the lady and her husband, whom she had met when she was fifteen, were able to fulfil her dream and buy the White House, as it was known. The day before the *Roadshow* came to Chartwell, some builders were removing an old water tank from her attic and it was then that she noticed an old piece of hardboard that had been used to lag the tank. Seeing Graham Sutherland's name and address on the outside, she looked at it more carefully and discovered that it was actually an unfinished painting by the artist. As she was already planning to go to the *Roadshow* with an old Victorian painting, which turned out to be of little value, she decided to take the Sutherland. As she said later: '*Somehow I felt that he meant for me to find the sketch at that moment.*'

Though best known today as a landscape artist who in the 1930s and during the Second World War explored the boundaries of landscape and abstraction – constantly relying on the inspiration he drew from the natural world – Sutherland was also a great portrait painter. However, some of his subjects were unhappy with the way that he depicted them. Most famously, Sir Winston Churchill hated the portrait of him that was painted by Sutherland to mark his eightieth birthday, and later Lady Churchill burned it. Sutherland's output, paintings, drawings, prints and illustrations, was prodigious, and included the design for the great *Christ in Glory* tapestry for the new Coventry Cathedral.

At Chartwell, overlooked by Sir Winston Churchill's house, Stephen Somerville was happy to confirm that the painting was indeed by Sutherland, and he gave it a value of £2,000–£3,000. Today, the painting still lives in Sutherland's former house, though it leaves from time to time to be shown in exhibitions.

# A LALIQUE VASE

---

*'We were going to bin it; we thought it was just a heap of junk.'*

The idea that an object, bought at a car boot fair for very little money, turns out to be an extremely valuable sleeper, has become the subject of urban myths. Sometimes, such stories can be taken with a pinch of salt yet, over the years, the *Roadshow* has thrown up many examples of objects that have turned out to be highly significant assets for their unsuspecting owners.

One such item was a glass vase that quickly became the subject of Eric Knowles' interest at Dumfries House in 2008. The owner had unearthed the object from the attic during a clear-out and brought it along to the show. She revealed that she had bought it at a car boot sale for a paltry £1 only because she liked the purple plant it contained. The plant eventually died and the vase was put away.

## A RARE DISCOVERY

As an expert on the decorative arts, especially Lalique glass, the *Roadshow's* Eric Knowles immediately recognised this small glass vase as the work of René Lalique (1860–1945).

Lalique is renowned as one of the twentieth century's pre-eminent glass designers and producers. As a young man, after studying at The Crystal Palace School of Art in Sydenham, he returned to France and designed pieces of jewellery for such eminent companies as Bucheron and Cartier. By 1885, Lalique had set up his own jewellery and glass designing business, becoming known for his groundbreaking use of low-value materials, such as horn, to create masterful and stunning pieces. One of Lalique's most celebrated creations – his Dragonfly 'lady' corsage of 1897–8 – was fashioned like gossamer from a mixture of gold, moonstones, chrysoprase, enamel and diamonds, and is displayed in the Calouste Gulbenkian Museum in Lisbon, Portugal.

By the 1920s, Lalique's reputation as a glassmaker had become synonymous with the Art Deco period. Ranging from architectural to domestic, his designs included the iconic first-class dining room for the famous *Normandie* ocean liner (and many other elements of the ship, too), fountains, church interiors, light shades, trinket boxes and light-up car mascots, all of which continually pushed back the boundaries for how glass could be used. The most iconic car mascot of all, *Spirit of the Wind*, is a beautiful personification of speed. Lalique's output was prodigious but even so, some pieces were technically more complicated and very rare.

Eric immediately knew that this lucky boot fair purchase fell into that category. His excitement was palpable as he explained that the 1929 piece – *Feuilles Fougères* – was made using a *cire perdue* or lost wax process, utilising a plaster mould, which made the piece unique. *'I've been waiting over twenty-five years for such an example to come into a* Roadshow', he said later. *'This was the stuff of dreams.'* As the tension mounted, Eric's humorous yet expertly proficient style built up to a mind-boggling valuation of £20,000. At just five inches high, the vase was one of the rarest and most valuable pieces of glass ever to appear on the *Antiques Roadshow*. *'We were going to bin it,'* said the owner, *'we thought it was a heap of junk'*. Luckily, they did not and, as a footnote to the story, it was later sent to a major London auction house, where it realized a commission-inclusive price of £32,450! That is not at all bad for a plant pot!

# DAMBUSTERS' PANDA MASCOT

When the *Roadshow* visited RAF Coningsby in 2015, the specialists hoped to find things connected to the history of aviation and, working with planes like the Lancaster, Spitfire and Hurricane in the background, they were not disappointed. However, what was not expected was an object that linked the *Roadshow* directly to the famous Dambusters Raid of May 1943, and 617 Squadron, based at nearby Scampton.

Memorabilia relating to the life of Flight Sergeant William Gordon Ratcliffe was brought in by his daughter and shown to militaria specialist, Mark Smith. Included with photographs, an RAF tunic and a DFC medal was, most significantly, the panda mascot that flew with Ratcliffe on sixty RAF missions over Germany, among them Operation Chastise, the dams raid. In times of war, small things brought from home or given by friends often achieved the status of mascots, and offered comfort and psychological support to their owners. Ratcliffe, a Canadian, was the flight engineer in the Lancaster bomber skippered by Joe McCarthy that attacked the Sorpe dam in the early hours of 23 May 1943, and the panda went with him as always, tucked into his boot. '*That's why one of his ears is worn down,*' his daughter explained. Well-known to all the crews he served with, the Ratcliffe panda worked hard to keep them all safe. Ratcliffe and his panda survived the war, but the flight engineer was killed in a car crash in Canada in 1952. His family then moved back to Britain, bringing the panda with them.

Today, the little panda is for Radcliffe's daughter a surviving link to the father she barely knew. '*He's been everywhere I haven't been and now I get to keep him safe,*' she explained. Faced with such a powerful reminder of aircrew life in the Second World War, Smith said: '*He was priceless to your dad, he is priceless to you, he is priceless to the RAF as a member of the Dams Raid crews. This little panda belongs to the nation.*'

# A PLANE SPOTTER'S
# NOTEBOOKS

*'It was amazing to have the chance to answer some of the questions about Glenn Miller's death and maybe solve one of the great mysteries of the Second World War.'*

Clive Stewart-Lockhart

There have been times when items brought into a *Roadshow* have actually changed history, usually by revealing information hitherto unknown. In these cases the information usually came from old documents that had either survived by chance within a family, or had never left that family.

On a hot and busy day at Hartland Abbey in North Devon in 2011, two notebooks compiled by a young plane enthusiast were brought in by his family. These revealed that during the latter part of the Second World War he had been a dedicated observer of aircraft movements, noting and precisely timing the passage of all aircraft that flew close to the family house near Reading or the airfield at Woodley, where the seventeen-year-old boy worked. His notes identified each aircraft, the direction of flight and estimated the altitude. His immensely detailed records offered an insight into the level of daily aircraft traffic over southern England at a late stage in the war.

## VALUABLE RECORDS

On 15 December 1944, the young planespotter noted the passage of an American UC-64A Norseman single-engine transport plane flying in a south-easterly direction across the horizon. At the time, it was just one among hundreds of similar entries. After his death years later, the notebooks passed to his brother, who kept them more in memory of his sibling than for the contents. However, when he had looked through them much later on, he had found a newspaper cutting tucked into the pages: *'He'd cut out an article from the Daily Express in 1969 about Glenn Miller's disappearance and he'd put it in the notebook's pages for 15 December 1944.'*

The loss of the great band leader Glenn Miller over the English Channel has always been one of the great unsolved mysteries of the Second World War. There have been many theories over the years ranging from the possible to the truly bizarre. However, by the late 1990s the most recent theory – that the Norseman had been downed by bombs jettisoned by a flight of Lancaster bombers returning from an aborted raid – had been widely accepted.

The only recorded sighting of the Norseman carrying Glenn Miller had been from Beachy Head, marking the point where the plane had crossed the English coast. With no other sightings

the plane's route could not be established and so it was felt that in the foggy conditions on that day the pilot could easily have drifted off his planned course, and into the route of the Lancasters. When he looked through the notebooks, and at that entry in particular, Clive Stewart-Lockhart knew that history could be changed for, if confirmed as genuine, the notebook entry revealed that when the Norseman passed by Reading, it was on course and on schedule. Clive could see from the notebooks that the young plane spotter had been totally dedicated to his hobby, and saw no reason to doubt the authenticity and accuracy of his very detailed notes.

## A PLAUSIBLE THEORY

After the programme had been broadcast, the new information was passed to the official Glenn Miller Archives in Colorado. They were initially sceptical, as they receive new theories about Miller's disappearance on an almost daily basis. However, when the organisation checked the known facts — such as the flight times, the plane's speed, the route and the weather — they realised that the young enthusiast had been correct and had seen the Norseman flying towards the south-east at about eight minutes past two on the afternoon of 15 December 1944. The Glenn Miller Archives then accepted the entry as a very valuable discovery and an important piece of the whole story, which obliterated not only the many theories about the plane going off course, but also made the jettisoned bombs idea impossible. This was because the Norseman, by sticking to its correct course, could not have coincided with the returning Lancasters. Since then, further research in America incorporating the evidence from the notebook has indicated that the cause of the Norseman's disappearance into the English Channel might have been icing in the carburettor, as a result of the freezing and foggy conditions that night.

Clive valued the notebooks for £1,000, but said that the information revealed was far more important. The family were very pleased: '*We're part of the Glenn Miller story, we're very thrilled about that.*'

# A WILLIAM BURGES BROOCH

Most *Roadshow* specialists have wish lists of things they would love to see one day, but they all know that these dreams are very rarely fulfilled. When the *Roadshow* visited Dartmouth in 2010, Geoffrey Munn revealed that top of his wish list was any jewellery designed by the great Victorian architect, William Burges. He explained that there were nine designs for brooches by Burges in the Victoria & Albert Museum, but nothing had ever been found that matched them.

An eagle-eyed viewer then contacted the BBC to say that she had a brooch somewhere that seemed to match one of the drawings. She was actually thinking about selling it, as it had been stuck in the bottom of a jewellery box for twenty years. She was invited to bring the brooch to a *Roadshow* at the end of that year's series, so that Geoffrey could see it. He was naturally very excited, and could hardly believe that that his dream had come true. '*It is definitely by Burges, and it hasn't been seen for over a hundred years.*'

Some jewellery by Burges is known, mainly because he was in the habit of commissioning special pieces as a kind of thank you for lady clients, or the wives of clients, and these have sometimes remained with the family. For example, important pieces were designed by him for Lady Bute. Burges was not alone among Victorian architects, artists and designers in creating jewellery, with notable examples by A. W. N. Pugin and the painter D. G. Rossetti.

Having been rescued from oblivion, the Burges brooch was subsequently sold at auction for £31,000. A year later an identical brooch appeared, and this one was bought by the Victoria & Albert Museum and so is now reunited with Burges' original design. It is now thought that the two brooches may have been made as presents for two bridesmaids and the initials found on the back may be those of the original donor.

# A STUMP WORK BOX

*'This is an exceptional box, of museum quality, that has probably been in the same house since it was new; that is, around 350 years.'*

John Foster

Britain is unusual in not having experienced invasion or serious political and social strife since the seventeenth century, and so many things have tended to remain in the same place. As a result, the *Roadshow* team are used to seeing, handling and discussing things that have been in the possession of one family for decades, if not centuries.

## AMAZING CONDITION

A remarkable example of this occured at Caversham in 2016, when a young man appeared with a seventeenth century box covered with embroidery. Examples of decorative needlework from that period are not particularly rare, and plenty have been seen at *Roadshows* over the years. However, these have generally been damaged and faded or in a broken or incomplete state, which is not surprising for objects that are over three hundred years old. The box that this young man brought in was very different and totally exceptional, as it looked at first sight to be almost brand new. The colours were bright, the details of the embroidery were all visible and John Foster could not understand how something of such quality had survived so long in that condition. He explained that the box demonstrated a mixture of techniques, including wool work, needlework and stump work, the last named being the sections stuffed with straw and other waste materials to give a raised effect, all of which were typical of the period.

## MILTON MANOR

The young man revealed that he was a guide at Milton Manor in Oxfordshire and the box had always been in the house. Everyone who saw it loved it, but he had brought it to the *Roadshow* to find out more about it. Milton Manor was built in the 1660s by the Carlton family, who had been major Berkshire landowners since the dissolution of monasteries in the sixteenth century. By the eighteenth century, the Carlton family fortunes had declined and Milton was sold in 1764 to Bryan Barrett, a wealthy London merchant who proceeded to rebuild the house in the Georgian style. His descendants still own the house he built, and its surrounding estates and have lived in it continuously, except for a short period when it was unoccupied and out of use.

It was following that time, when the family were making the house habitable again, that the box was found in a former servant's bedroom, wrapped in brown paper and an old tablecloth.

## AN EXCEPTIONAL PIECE

For John, this explained how the box had survived in such good condition, hidden away, out of the light, and never handled, possibly over decades. He saw the box as a great discovery, something that could have been part of the contents of the original seventeenth century house. Its chance survival offered an unexpected insight into the domestic life and attitudes of the Restoration period. The embroidered decoration on the box told various stories, including those of Solomon and the Queen of Sheba, Sarah and Isaac and Hagar and Ishmael – typical of the Biblical themes that were popular at the time. Also typical were the animals and flowers, though much more unusual were the seed pearl details and the carved wooden hands of the embroidered figures.

## A POLITICAL STATEMENT

John explained that, apart from the obvious love symbolism, there was an underlying political message. Milton was built by a Royalist family celebrating the return of the monarchy, and its contents would have supported that message. The box, as part of that, was also a political statement which would have been easily understood at the time. *'This is a lady's toilet box, and the embroidery, with its joint themes of love and support for the monarchy, could well have been made by the ladies of Milton Manor. It is an exceptional piece, of museum quality, and would be worth £50,000 to £70,000 if it were ever to be sold. But, having been in the same house for over three hundred years, I hope that never happens.'*

# TITANIC LETTER

After the *Titanic* disaster in 1912, the world was flooded with commemorative items and souvenirs, including special newspapers and magazines, memorial cards and postcards – even memorial paper napkins. Examples are often seen at *Roadshow*s and the owners are sometimes disappointed by the relatively low values quoted, which are a reflection of the large numbers of items produced. On the other hand, letters and postcards written by people on board the *Titanic* are always much more poignant, very rare, and thus highly desirable.

On her maiden voyage, the *Titanic*'s last port of call on 11 April 1912 before setting off into the north Atlantic was Queenstown in southern Ireland. 1,395 bags of mail were loaded, along with 123 passengers, while a few bags of mail written by passengers and crew on board the ship were taken ashore for posting. Many of these letters and cards were destined to be delivered after the ship had sunk and inevitably some had been written by people who did not survive the disaster. The arrival of mail from a lost loved one must have been hard to bear. Inevitably, a number of those letters and cards still exist and their content is often similar: brief descriptions of the ship and its lavish interiors, optimism about the voyage and anticipation of the forthcoming experience of America, and sadness at leaving family and friends.

A typical *Titanic* letter surfaced at a *Roadshow* in Hull in 1997: a single sheet, written on both sides and headed by the White Star line's badge. It was written by John Harper, a Glasgow Baptist minister on his way to become a missionary in Chicago, to the owner's great-grandmother, the caretaker of his former church. In the letter, he addresses her as Mother Superior, which was apparently his nickname for her. The letter is typical of so many sent from the ship – friendly, relaxed, full of hope for the voyage and his future life in America. John Harper did not survive.

The letter was not in good condition, much folded and mended on the back with sticky tape. However, Paul Atterbury still valued it at £2,000. Since then, the *Titanic* market has grown hugely, helped by films and other media coverage and by the travelling exhibition of artefacts raised from the ship. Collectors are desperate to find things that are clearly associated with the ship, and letters posted from the *Titanic* have risen in value accordingly. The family still have the letter, though it is currently on loan to the *Titanic* Museum in Belfast. They have been advised that it is now worth £25,000.

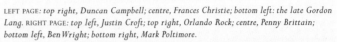

LEFT PAGE: *top right, Duncan Campbell; centre, Frances Christie; bottom left: the late Gordon Lang.* RIGHT PAGE: *top left, Justin Croft; top right, Orlando Rock; centre, Penny Brittain; bottom left, Ben Wright; bottom right, Mark Poltimore.*

# A SAXON GOLD RING

<hr>

*'This ring will always be one of the most memorable of my* Roadshow *finds. It is an emblem of our national identity.'*

Geoffrey Munn

Some *Roadshow* discoveries seem to catch the public's imagination and live on long after the actual progamme of which they were part has been forgotten. One of these is a gold ring that was brought to Houghton Hall in 2001 and seen by Geoffrey Munn.

The owner described how he had found it while clearing away some hedge clippings in his Norfolk garden. *'I only saw it because it was glinting in the sun. My wife thought it was something that might have come from a Christmas cracker. I thought it was old so I reported it to the police.'* For Geoffrey, it was a memorable moment, for he knew he was looking at an Anglo-Saxon gold ring, probably from the eighth century.

## ANCIENT TREASURE

The Anglo-Saxons, made up largely of various invading Germanic tribes, dominated England from the end of the Roman era in the fifth century to the Norman invasion in 1066. Initially warring and competing tribes controlled England, gradually establishing six kingdoms – Northumbria, Mercia, East Anglia, Kent, Sussex and Wessex, all of which were finally united in 927 by King Aethelstan. Traditionally, the Anglo-Saxon period had been seen as unstable, with the spread of Christianity challenging established religions, and the country facing invasions by Vikings, Danes and other settlers. For this reason, it was known to historians as the Dark Ages. However, recent research has challenged that perception, indicating that the Anglo-Saxon centuries were actually marked by social advances and high levels of creativity, with the latter being notably marked by metalwork and jewellery. Great national treasures like the Sutton Hoo ship burial had long established this at a royal level, but it is only recently that a broader understanding of Anglo-Saxon society as a whole has been developed, thanks in part to discoveries such as the Staffordshire hoard of 3,500 pieces of fragmented gold jewellery and metalwork found in 2009.

Geoffrey well understood the significance of the gold ring and the story it could tell. He called it: *'A silent witness to a very remote, very sparse episode of human existence.'* He continued: *'Gold, like the earth and every earthly element, is born of the sun and its colour recalls its fiery origins. It is*

*ductile and extremely malleable, the properties that allowed this Saxon ring to be made a millennium ago from plaited wires of pure gold. It was certainly made for a high-ranking person, perhaps even a king. It is easy to imagine him galloping across the East Anglian plains in the winter winds when the ring fell from his finger. There it remained, lost, until the present owner found it in the hedge. Gold is incorruptible and so it emerged into the sunlight as if it had been made only yesterday.'*

## TREASURE TROVE ANALYSIS

Having reported his find to the police, the owner went through the long Treasure Trove procedures that apply to antiquities discovered by excavation or by chance. The ring was out of his possession for a year but in the end the inquest reported that he could keep it as originally it had been lost, not hidden.

Geoffrey valued the ring for £10,000, but now thinks it could be worth double that, while adding: *'These sums do not reflect the magic of this ring which above all is an emblem of our national identity.'*

# A TOURMALINE RING

The technical definition of an antique is something that is a hundred years old, but today that definition is rarely applied, particularly at the *Roadshow*. During the course of a *Roadshow* day, the expert team will see many things that are certainly not antiques, but are often very interesting nonetheless. Modern design has often been featured, in ceramics and glass, in furniture and interior decoration, in costume and notably in silver and jewellery. Joanna Hardy, one of the show's jewellery experts, is well known for her enthusiasm for contemporary jewellery, and so she was excited by a ring brought into the *Roadshow* at Audley End in 2015 by a mother and daughter.

Their main reason for coming had been to find out about a pearl necklace. The mother explained that it had originally been given to her mother-in-law when her husband had been born. The pearls then had been passed to her daughter who said, '*I've never worn them but they are special to all of us because Mum wore them on my wedding day.*' However, they had also brought along a ring, and it was this that caught Joanna's eye.

In the 1960s a new style of jewellery appeared, inspired by natural textures and abstract forms. A leading figure was Andrew Grima, whose shop in London's Jermyn Street was at the heart of this jewellery revolution. Many other designers followed his lead, including Lawrence Wheaton, who was associated with Collingswood, a retailer in Conduit Street. Joanna felt that this ring, which featured a large green tourmaline and four diamonds in a gold setting inspired by marine life, might be by Wheaton – but it was not hall-marked. The owner, the mother, told Joanna that she had bought the ring in 1972, using money she had received in settlement of an insurance claim for a stolen diamond brooch. Having talked about the revolutionary nature of the jewellery of that era, Joanna valued the ring for £5,000 to £7,000.

Later, the story was followed up by Joanna at Goldsmiths' Hall, where she was able to show the owner Lawrence Wheaton's original design for the ring, and then arranged to have the ring properly hall-marked.

# A SILVER DUCK
# CLARET JUG

The nineteenth century was a great period for the production of luxury goods, thanks to an ever-expanding consumer market as the wealth generated by industry and trade worked its way through the system. It was a good time to be a silversmith, particularly for those specialising in novelty wares. Cruet sets, pepper pots, vesta cases, pin cushions, menu holders, card cases and many other luxury domestic wares were in demand, and perennially popular were those featuring animals and birds.

Well used to seeing such things at *Roadshows*, Ian Pickford was nonetheless surprised and delighted when an unusual duck-shaped claret jug was brought in to the Dorking *Roadshow* in 1998. He knew at once that it had been made by Alexander Crichton.

Surprisingly little is known about this Victorian silversmith, though he appears to have had Scottish roots. His earliest known work dates from the 1870s, but it was in the early 1880s that he really made his name as the designer and maker of novelty claret jugs in animal and bird forms, made distinctive by their combination of glass and silver. Over thirty designs were produced by him between 1881 and 1882, many of which were registered at the Patent Office. For a while, Crichton was in partnership with John Curry, with a workshop and showroom in London's Oxford Street. The list of animal and bird models is extensive and includes owls, parrots, penguins, cockatoos, walruses, dodos, crocodiles and carp. He also made other animal table items, such as lighters and honeypots. Affected by the severe recession of the mid-1880s, Crichton went bankrupt in 1886.

The owners had inherited their duck claret jug and, when told it was worth £950, they had wrapped it up and put it away in a trunk. Friends who had long admired it had persuaded them to get it out and bring it to the *Roadshow*. Having pointed out the remarkable details of the engraving on the glass body and the quality of the modelling of the silver, Ian told them that it was an extremely rare survivor from an age of luxury and indulgence. He explained; '*Novelty claret jugs are always in demand today, but this one is something special. The combination of Crichton as the maker and the duck shape makes this exceptionally desirable.*' To the owners' amazement, he then valued the jug for £25,000.

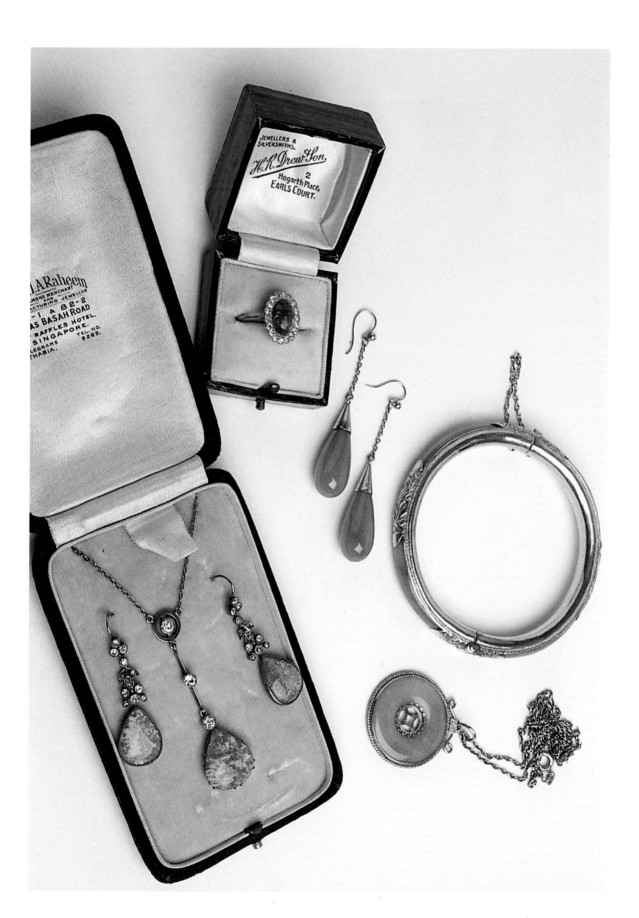

# THE REFUSE TIP JEWELLERY

The *Roadshow*'s visit to Cliveden in 2001 was memorable in many ways, not least thanks to the backdrop of the house and its extraordinary political history. However, this was also the setting for one of the *Roadshow*'s most unusual, and enduringly popular finds.

A lady and her son appeared, laden with boxes and bags of assorted jewellery and, when she was filmed in conversation with John Benjamin, she revealed that everything she had brought in had been found by her in other people's rubbish. For seventeen years she had been in charge of a local tip and, in return for a modest fee, she had been granted salvage rights. She explained how, over the years, she had rescued the jewellery by digging deep into rubbish bags and by examining things that others would not touch. John, visibly struggling as he tried to keep up with her story, said: '*So, let me get it right, everything on the table had been thrown away.*' She told him how a refuse tip worked and how many people threw away things without checking them, particularly if they were clearing a house.

John then discussed the pieces that were spread out on the table, identifying ear-rings, pendants, rings and brooches, some made from jade and opals, and others from silver and gold. Some were still in their original boxes, looking as though they had never been worn since they were bought in the 1920s and 1930s. The lady explained to John that what she had brought into the show that day was just a fraction of what she had stored at home. As John went through the items again, giving individual values, the lady turned to her son and said: '*Find yourself a girl and you can have these.*' The total valuation came in at between £4,000 and £6,000.

With its combination of an extraordinary and unexpected story, the excitement of things of value thrown away as worthless, an owner full of character, and a specialist cleverly and calmly leading her on until it was time to take control, this item quickly became a *Roadshow* classic, and has been much repeated ever since.

Sadly, the story does not have a happy ending. The lady retired from the tip some years ago and since then has suffered from ill health, which she thinks is the result of her not being out in the open every day. Her son, still unmarried, now owns a pub. Some of the jewellery was sold, but for prices below the original valuations.

# AN ENGLISH
# MARQUETRY
# COMMODE

In its early years, great examples of British and European furniture appeared frequently on the *Roadshow*. However, now such things are rarely seen. Indeed, it is not uncommon today for shows to be broadcast which do not feature any furniture at all. This change, like so many that have affected the *Roadshow* over its long life, reflects changes in taste and fashion. It is also to do with changing attitudes to collecting, and to eighteenth century furniture as a whole, which is nowadays often dismissed under the all-embracing name of 'brown furniture'. At the same time, really important examples have become much rarer.

In 1984, when the *Roadshow* visited Douglas in the Isle of Man, John Bly described an eighteenth century commode brought to the show as '*the most important piece that I have ever seen on the* Roadshow'. Since then, John has seen other pieces of equal importance, but this commode has probably never been eclipsed.

In the eighteenth century English cabinet making came of age. This was largely due to the arrival in Britain from the late seventeenth century onwards of generations of European craftsmen, who were often fleeing religious and political upheaval, and who brought with them European techniques and styles. The most influential countries were Holland and France, and from them came new constructional techniques, new and more colourful styles of marquetry and gilded bronze mounts, along with the Rococo style. At first sight, this bombe-shaped commode looked French, but John Bly was quick to establish that it was in fact English, made in the reign of George III and dating from around 1773. He could not attribute it to a particular maker, though names such as John Cobb, William Vile and Pierre Langlois were in the frame.

As John explored the sophistication of the construction, the superb quality of the marquetry, the range of woods used and the detail of the bronze mounts, he made it clear that he was looking at something remarkable. Indeed, this was a very rare survivor from a great, but still under-appreciated period of English cabinet making. John also noted the use of a new technique to improve the detail of the marquetry: '*In the seventeenth century, details such as the veining on leaves was done by cutting through the veneers with a fine saw. In the eighteenth century, the details were etched onto the surface of the veneer and so did not penetrate the wood, another instance of European influence. The detail is much finer but with time it can wear and lose its sharpness, as on this commode.*'

The owners, who lived on a farm, knew little about the commode and had no idea of its importance. Their mother had been in service and had been given it after the death of one of her employers. As a result the commode, which had been in daily use, was not looking its best, much of the detail hidden beneath layers of dirt and polish. However, it was in one piece and was not in need of significant restoration. To the astonishment of the owners, John valued the commode for over £30,000 and this seemed at the time a high price. However, when it appeared later on the market, it was sold for £50,000.

# MARGARET CALKIN JAMES, POSTER DESIGNER

*'Although lots of people out there may not know Margaret Calkin James's name they certainly should, as she was an important designer, particularly in the poster field. I was glad to have the chance to help put another lady artist on the map.'*

Hilary Kay

Posters, especially those relating to travel, are always popular with both collectors and *Roadshow* audiences because they are often bright and colourful, and have an obvious nostalgic appeal. However, because posters were essentially ephemeral, surviving examples in good condition are rare. The modern full-colour poster emerged at the end of the nineteenth century, thanks largely to the development of new printing techniques and coinciding with the emergence of modern advertising ideas and styles. From the start, artists were drawn to posters and poster design and many companies were glad to exploit this, knowing that their presence on the high street depended upon strong and immediately recognisable images. Some poster artists and designers were either well known at the time, or have subsequently become well known, helped by an increasing interest in the history of graphic design and advertising. Despite that, there are many poster artists whose names are unfamiliar or unknown today, partly because many images were either left unsigned or marked only with a monogram or initials, which are often untraceable now.

## DESERVED RECOGNITION

At Coughton Court in 2005, Hilary Kay was able to fill one of these gaps when she was confronted by a large collection of posters and other decorative graphic work brought in to the *Roadshow* by the family of a lady named Margaret Calkin James.

Born in London in 1895, one of seven children, Margaret Calkin was a typical product of her age and greatly influenced by the philosophies of the Arts & Crafts movement. She attended the Central School of Art and later Westminster School of Art, learning watercolour painting, print making, calligraphy, textile design and printing, as well as other skills that enabled her to work as a graphic artist. In 1920, she opened the Rainbow Workshops in Bloomsbury, central London – the first gallery set up by a woman to promote and sell art, craft and design, including her own work. In 1922, Margaret Calkin married an architect, Charles Holloway James, adding

his surname to her maiden name. Throughout the 1920s and 1930s, she practised as a graphic designer, and her output included book jackets for publishers, pattern papers for the Curwen Press, programmes and booklets for the BBC, and the first greetings telegram for the GPO. She worked in styles that placed her firmly within the British design avant garde, alongside names such as McKnight Kauffer and Rex Whistler. In 1938, she also designed textiles for Norwich City Hall – in itself a famous modernist statement. However, Calkin James' main claim to fame was as a poster designer, for London Transport and the Southern Railway, both companies that were famous for their commitment to modern design, and with a shared vision of the poster as a marriage of modern art and industry. Her daughter remembered her excitement at seeing her mother's work on the walls of underground stations in London.

## A GREAT BODY OF WORK

The collection brought to the *Roadshow* included posters and other graphic work, sketches and designs and diaries and daybooks. All these together offered an insight not only into Calkin James's work but also into the role of women in an industry that was largely dominated by men during her lifetime. Hilary Kay suggested that this could be one of the reasons why her work is not better known today, outside the fairly narrow world of poster collecting, though she knew that Calkin James' work was well represented in the collections of the Victoria & Albert Museum. When it came to values, Hilary suggested that the better-known posters, particularly those for London Transport, could each be worth a few hundred pounds, while the whole collection could certainly be priced in four figures.

# A WILLIAM KENT
# STYLE TABLE

For many – both the viewers and those working on the programme – the *Antiques Roadshow* can be a valuable guide to style history. Objects often reflect the times in which they were made and used, and a good interpreter can use them to bring those times to life. This massive side table, which was brought into the Colchester *Roadshow* in 1994, was used in this way by furniture specialist Deborah Lambert to explore the style history of early eighteenth century Britain. Found by the owner in a Hampshire junk shop in the 1950s, it had been attributed to William Kent.

Kent – architect, interior decorator, landscape gardener and furniture designer – was a key figure in the formation of the taste for the Palladian style in the Britain of the 1730s and 1740s. Having spent some years in Italy, Kent returned to Britain filled with ideas drawn from both the classical world and from the Renaissance styles associated with Andrea Palladio, in time to help establish neo-Palladianism as the style of choice for a new generation of wealthy country house builders. He was, therefore, a crucial figure in the shaping of Georgian Britain. A man of exceptional talent and vision, he designed houses and their contents, and even the State Coach, all in the characteristically heavy, ornate and extravagantly classical style that he helped to make fashionable.

As a style leader, Kent was very influential, and so the challenge for Deborah was to establish whether this richly carved side table with its marble top was actually by Kent or a lesser, and probably anonymous, follower. She started with the base, which was carved from pine and would originally have been richly gilded, and explained that a piece such as this would have been made, perhaps as a pair, to grace the hall of a large country house. She then traced the source of the sphinx-like figure supports to ancient Rome, where frescoes depicting figures that combined animal, human and plant forms had been excavated in the fifteenth century, copied by Raphael in the Renaissance, and then brought to northern Europe by artists such as Berain in the seventeenth century. She continued: '*Kent's sphinxes, taken from engravings after Berain, were perfectly proportioned, as were their Roman sources. These ones have huge heads, matronly busts and very puny hind quarters. And while Kent was known for his massive eagle supports, this strange bird is half swan, half eagle.*' As a result, Deborah was able to say that the table had probably been made by an unknown follower of Kent at some point in the first half of the eighteenth century. '*It might have been bought by someone keen to be seen to be following the contemporary taste for classicism, but more concerned about the look than the details.*'

Nonetheless, as a side table in the William Kent manner that dated from the early eighteenth century, the item was still valued for £15,000 – a highly significant increase on the £60 that the owner had paid for it forty years earlier.

LEFT PAGE: *top, queuing in the rain; centre left, Philip Hook and Henry Wyndham, former picture boys; centre right, a Marilyn moment; bottom left, Highclere Castle aka Downton Abbey; bottom right, jukebox at Wimbledon.* RIGHT PAGE: *top left, the Roadshow bike; top centre, Ian Harris; top right, Keith Baker; centre left, Portmeirion at Portmeirion; bottom, Barbara Cartland's hats.*

# AN AUDEMARS PIGUET WATCH

A good wristwatch brings together technical excellence with dateless style and elegance, and over the years the *Roadshow* has highlighted many exceptional examples of this combination. A particularly memorable one appeared at Stowmarket in 1990, when a couple brought in a long black case containing a watch made by Audemars Piguet. They had treasured it for years and, knowing it to be a watch of rare quality, they said they expected it to be worth £5,000.

Founded in Switzerland in 1875 by two talented young watchmakers, Jules-Louis Audemars and Eduard-Auguste Piguet, the Audemars Piguet company was established to produce watch movements of exceptional quality and precision. Their first wristwatches were produced in the first decade of the twentieth century – including an early minute repeater dating from 1907 – and from that point their reputation grew by leaps and bounds until the 1920s and 1930s, when the company attained the pre-eminence that it still enjoys today.

Wristwatches first became popular during the First World War, due to the difficulty of using pocket watches in modern warfare. In warfare, the need to know the time had to be answered immediately and getting a watch out of a uniform pocket took too long and often required the use of both hands. At first, fob, or small pocket watches were given strap fittings to enable them to be worn on the wrist, but manufacturers soon began making standard wristwatches. By the time the war ended, the wristwatch habit was well established. At the same time, the wristwatch, because of its visibility on the wrist, became a fashion statement whose importance went far beyond the simple needs of timekeeping.

This watch was made in the 1930s and is redolent of elegant Art Deco styling. It is a minute repeater in a white gold case, and was manufactured for Gubelin Lucerne, a family firm of Swiss jewellers that was famous for selling high-quality watches. Several things make this watch special, including the one-off rectangular and ultra-slim case, the complexity of the movement with its repeating facility and the quality of its design and construction. These were all hallmarks of the best Audemars Piguet watches of that period. After he had examined it carefully, Simon Bull said that there was probably no other watch in the world quite like it.

Aware that the owners believed their watch to be worth £5,000, Simon simply told them they could add a nought to their valuation. The following year, this watch was sold for £57,000.

# AN EIGHTEENTH-CENTURY DRESS

*'I knew I was looking at something truly remarkable.'*  Hilary Kay

Over the years, the *Antiques Roadshow* has featured many different items of designer fashion from different decades of the twentith century – the 1930s (flapper dresses), suits from the 1940s, 1960s and 1970s, as well as theatrical costumes – but rarely has an article of clothing from the eighteenth century made an appearance. So few items from this era survive intact and those that do are often in very poor condition. However, this is not always the case, as the show at Tewkesbury Abbey in 2016 was to prove.

Plastic bags are a common feature of *Roadshow* queues and the experts often wonder what treasures may be lurking inside them. For George Archdale and Hilary Kay, the day at Tewkesbury – and a plastic bag – produced one of the most remarkable pieces of period costume ever discovered at a *Roadshow* venue. Although the prospect of something interesting coming to their table is exciting, our experts usually defer to each other's differing fields of expertise. Seeing a bagful of finely decorated silk, George knew immediately that Hilary should take a look. Sure enough, Hilary's heart *'skipped a beat'* as the material turned out to be none other than an embroidered and painted dress dating from around the 1760s, which had been given as a present to the owner and stored in a plastic bag for fifty years.

## EXOTIC STYLE

Known as a *'robe à la Française'* or 'sack-back gown', this distinctive style of dress has fabric cascading from the shoulders and arranged in box or 'Watteau' pleats – named after Antoine Watteau, whose paintings feature many such dresses. The 'Tewkesbury dress' (as it became known) was made of silk and would have been worn with a fancy stomacher and bolstered with hoops and paniers. In the eighteenth century, Europeans had become fascinated by Eastern cultures, and fashions made in the Turquerie, Indiennerie, Chinoiserie and Egyptian styles were highly prized between the late seventeenth and early nineteenth centuries. The silk was largely painted in China – itself a complicated process. Raw silk is non-absorbent and requires sizing with a cured solution of glue and alum to provide a stable surface for painting. Storage in a plastic bag for several decades is not normally the best way to preserve any precious fabric, let alone a fragile eighteenth century dress, yet Hilary was astounded by the near mint condition of the gown and *'felt the hair on the back of* [her] *neck rise!'*

The survival rate of 250-year-old fabric is very small indeed. Usually, it deteriorates over time, eaten away by the acids used in the size and the paint as well as by insects. Additionally, valuable fabrics were frequently reused and the dresses were re-styled or even thrown into dressing-up boxes. In front of the cameras, the owner – a lovely lady aged around eighty years old and the unwitting custodian of a textile treasure – was completely astounded to hear, for the very first time, about the history of the dress and its great age. When Hilary revealed the value, an extraordinary £40,000, there was an audible gasp from the audience.

## A POTENTIAL MUSEUM PIECE

Such items are rarely seen outside major museums and both Hilary and the owner visited the Victoria & Albert Museum to compare the Tewkesbury dress with other similar period pieces. Susan North, the museum's senior curator, agreed that it was an important example of its kind. At the time of writing, the dress is currently in the hands of a specialist agent and could end up in a museum or private collection. Whatever the final outcome, this *Roadshow* item is certainly one that neither Hilary nor George will ever forget.

# STATUS QUO TAPESTRY

Many emotive stories have been featured on the *Roadshow* over the years, and specialists sometimes have to handle situations with a greater degree of sensitivity than usual. While filming the show at Tredegar House in 2014, miscellaneous expert Marc Allum was confronted by a large woolwork tapestry made as a tribute to the famous rock band Status Quo. As the story unfolded, it became clear that the lady being interviewed was the mother of a boy who had – at the age of eighteen – been involved in a serious motorcycle accident. Very sadly, this had left him paralysed from the neck downwards and unable to use his fingers, although he did have some slight movement in his arms. Marc struggled to hold back the tears, but as the conversation progressed, the relevance of the Status Quo tapestry became clear. After five years, the son, who was '*Status Quo mad*', gained a little more movement and began making this large tapestry as a tribute to his favourite band.

With the aid of a rotating frame, he worked from his wheelchair, using his teeth to 'sew' the huge woolwork, which was taller than Marc himself! An emotionally moved Marc pointed out details in the work including the references to the band members, song titles and their chart positions. Very poignantly, he also noted that the bottom of the tapestry remained unfinished. Having lived, against all the odds, until the age of thirty-nine, the young man died before he could finish his great work. His mother, who had loved and looked after him, was immensely proud but clearly found it an ordeal to talk about him publicly. A testament to his endurance and patience, the tapestry naturally had pride of place in his mother's home. For once, Marc deliberately chose not to mention any value other than its precious status within the family.

As with so many items on the *Roadshow*, the story does not end there. Interest in the piece snowballed, to the point that it reached the ears of Status Quo, who kindly invited Marc and the owner to Shepperton Studios, where they were rehearsing for their forthcoming European tour. Band members Francis Rossi and Rick Parfitt broke from their playing to chat and look at the piece, and were obviously moved by the devotion that had gone into making it. As a fitting tribute and with the owner's permission, they 'completed' the unfinished area at the bottom of the tapestry by signing it. It was both a sad and happy moment for all involved. The meeting was aired on a Christmas special and Marc described it as a '*fitting and emotional tribute*' to someone who had endured a great deal. He was also pleased as punch because Francis Rossi let him play

his famous bottle-green Fender Telecaster, a veteran instrument of the rock world. To quote a Status Quo song, 'The Power of Rock' inspired an unlucky but courageous young man to carry on. The *Roadshow* was able to tell his story. (With the greatest of respect to Rick Parfitt, who passed away in 2016.)

# LAWRENCE OF ARABIA'S WATCH

Wristwatches have been a growth area for collectors and investors for a long time. The core market tends to be very male orientated. In a way, that is not surprising – many men are attracted to the mechanics and history of watches, or the style of timepieces sold by such prestige companies as Breguet, Patek Philippe and Jaeger LeCoultre. They also dream of owning a piece worn by James Bond or one that has been 'space-flown' on the wrist of a famous astronaut. What is certain, though, is that watch values have rocketed in recent decades.

*Antiques Roadshow*'s clocks and watches table sees the odd gem amongst the usual horde of unremarkable but well-loved watches and timepieces. At the Barnstaple show in 1986, expert Simon Bull was shown a silver-cased Omega chronograph that had been purchased in a Newport (South Wales) market twenty years earlier. Having initially paid around £70 or £80 for it, plus another £10 on repairs, the owner had effectively acquired a good-looking watch worth around £1,500–£2,000 – a lucky purchase. Unusually though, this watch had a large 'A' over an arrow engraved on the back, denoting it as British Army issue, as well as an original guarantee slip dated 1933. Simon was quick to realise that the name on the slip was T. E. Shaw, the pseudonym of Thomas Edward Lawrence, better known as Lawrence of Arabia. For most people, the name conjures up images of Peter O'Toole in his famous role as the maverick soldier and spy who played a major role in the Arab uprising against the Ottoman Empire during the First World War. As with any provenance, this possible association opened up a whole host of issues regarding the actual history of the watch. A typical *Roadshow* day does not often allow time for in-depth research into an object before filming. Instead, it is down to the expert's knowledge and (sometimes) innate intuition. However, Simon knew that he could be looking at an incredibly historic watch and valued it at £5,000, albeit with a few caveats.

After the programme featuring the watch had aired, collectors and forums eagerly discussed its likely origins. According to Omega archives, the serial number on the movement – 4'428'513 – showed that it had been ordered 'by France or one of its colonies' in 1915, whereas the back of the case (caseback) had a different serial number – 4'789'731 – corresponding to a standard watch ordered in 1912 by a Liverpool retailer. The caseback had also been altered by hand to accommodate the larger chronograph movement. Such idiosyncrasies remain unexplained, making some sceptics doubt the provenance of the watch. However, when the watch was offered for auction in 2000, it realised the reassuring equivalent of £33,800, casting aside any doubts about its authenticity. The buyer was the Omega Museum in Biel, Switzerland, where it is currently exhibited – a fitting home for an historic wristwatch and a great *Roadshow* horological find.

# A DIAMOND
# BUTTERFLY BROOCH

The language of jewellery is both intriguing and beguiling. The hidden messages encapsulated within the stones and symbolic constructions of flowers, animals and insects can leave *Roadshow* jewellery specialists eulogising far more than any other items. Expert John Benjamin is well known for his effervescent style and in 2001 his enthusiasm was evident when he was presented with an attractive diamond brooch, at a Wimbledon *Roadshow* in the form of a moth – or was it a butterfly?

Clearly less squeamish than we are now, the Victorians were particularly keen on jewellery fashioned in the form of insects. Literally everything – from parasols to veils and bonnets – would be decorated with all types of iridescent beetles and flies. More expensive and individual pieces would often be festooned with spiders and bees. Dating from the early twentieth century, this particular brooch had been left to the owner in around 1958, having originally been bought as a present by her uncle for his wife. The Edwardian brooch was lavishly furnished with six large diamonds, one on each wing and two on the body, surrounded by a myriad of smaller diamonds. The entire effect was spectacular. John's comments about the design, and the notion that it may be a moth rather than a butterfly, created some joviality, but the tone soon became more serious as he built up to the valuation in his own inimitable way. A master of brinkmanship, John then left the owner stunned by his £60,000 insurance valuation that, by anyone's estimation, is considerable. Butterflies – by the way – are more desirable than moths!

As is often the case, media comment led to speculation about the retailer's mark in the original box, a small printed black cartouche with the name of Linden & Co., New Bond Street, London. It transpired that the business had originally been set up by the great-uncle of the present owner who is still in business under the same name. It had thrived under his great-uncle's direction after Britain came off the Gold Standard in 1931, providing opportunities to trade the precious metal more advantageously. '*We probably know a thing or two about silver and jewellery*' said the owner, '*and butterfly brooches are still very popular*'. The brooch remains in the family.

# A STEIFF CLOWN BEAR

Well known to millions of *Roadshow* viewers, Steiff is a brand that is synonymous with valuable teddy bears. Founded in 1880 in Germany by Margarete Steiff, the company began by making animal-shaped pincushions. It soon expanded into the children's market with a selection of other creatures including pigs, dogs and cats. In 1902, Steiff launched the bear, said to have been called the teddy bear after the American president Theodore 'Teddy' Roosevelt. Sales soared when the bears were introduced to America four years later. During that time, the company may have sold almost a million bears worldwide. Success also gave other manufacturers the incentive to copy Steiff's products. To discourage the production of counterfeit bears, Franz, one of Margarete's nephews, came up with the ingenious idea of putting a metal button in the ear. This novel trademark has become almost as famous as the bears themselves. Nowadays, Steiff still makes the bears, alongside a large variety of other animals. Of course, some are much rarer than others and, every now and again, a real gem crops up at a *Roadshow* event.

One such standout teddy materialised at Mount Stewart House, Northern Ireland, in 2003. It bore all the obvious hallmarks of a Steiff, but without any button in the ear. Miscellaneous expert Marc Allum had just sat down at his table to greet the first customer of the day when they produced the aforementioned bear. It was immediately distinctive as a Steiff Teddy Clown. Without saying anything to the owners, Marc immediately popped over to his colleague, Bunny Campione, who knows her stuff when it comes to bears.

It's not often that your first object of the day turns out to be a potential headline puller. Bunny later filmed the bear with its owners, who professed to have kept it in the bag for forty years. She explained how the Teddy Clown was produced in limited numbers during the mid-1920s. Complete with pointed conical felt hat and purple-trimmed ruff, these adorable bears are firm favourites amongst serious collectors. The condition was good; despite a couple of moth holes and some dust, the curly mohair with brown tips had not thinned to the usual 'well loved' condition of so many bears. Apparently, the button had been removed from his ear to keep it safe, but since his growler did not work, Teddy had effectively also lost his voice! Bunny gradually built up to a heart-stopping valuation of £20,000, leaving the owner stunned. The bear had already been valued locally for £3,000, but a second opinion at the *Roadshow* proved itself worth queuing for. Teddy was subsequently offered for auction in London in December 2003, making a premium-inclusive £23,500.

# THE HIROSHIMA
# BOWLS

*Roadshow* objects are often connected to major events in history. Artefacts associated with war, suffering or individual heroism paint vivid pictures of the best and worst of human nature, which is what makes the *Roadshow* so interesting.

At the Torquay show in 1999, well-known orientalist Lars Tharp was intrigued by a group of nesting Japanese ceramic bowls. Unusually, the bowls were fused together as if they had failed in the kiln, a situation technically known as a 'kiln waster' and not uncommon in pottery production. This situation occurs at high temperatures when the glaze runs, gluing the pieces together. However, as Lars coaxed the story from the owner, it became clear that kiln waster was not to blame this time. What had fused the bowls together was not the heat of a kiln, but an atomic bomb. The bowls were from Hiroshima.

There are few words to describe the scale of death, misery and destruction produced by the dropping of atomic bombs on the Japanese cities of Hiroshima and Nagasaki on 6 and 9 August 1945. At least 130,000 people are thought to have perished, either as a direct result of the bomb blasts or in the months that followed from acute burns, radiation sickness and starvation. Although the rights and wrongs of President Harry S. Truman's decision to drop the bombs will forever be debated, he was faced with a nation that would not surrender. With no apparently viable alternative to demonstrate the power of the bomb effectively enough to stop the war without casualties, the resulting destruction was a foregone conclusion. As these thoughts no doubt passed through his head, Lars pondered over these bowls – such modest vessels and yet such powerful symbols of a cataclysmic event that changed the world forever. '*How do you put a value on these?*' he asked. '*They simply record an extraordinary moment in time.*'

Interestingly, in 2006 Lars was faced with a comparable situation when the show filmed at Norwich Cathedral. A visitor to the show, whose relative, a doctor, was one of the first Britons to enter Hiroshima after the bombing, showed some pieces of pottery that were discoloured in a similar way to those in Torquay. One item was, in fact, an English-made bowl, the other a Japanese piece, but both had irrefutably been coloured by the heat of the fireball, giving them a purple hue. As Lars said, the objects were an '*eloquent testimony to a moment when the world changed*'.

# THE GREAT TRAIN ROBBERS' MONOPOLY SET

It is the bestselling game in the world – the vast majority of us will have played *Monopoly* at some point in our lives. The game was invented in America during the early twentieth century by Elizabeth Magie, by all accounts an ardent anti-monopolist. Her original, more educational version – *The Landlord's Game* – highlighted the danger of property and land falling into the hands of powerful monopolies. Eventually, after several changes and copyright issues, it became the property of Parker Brothers and the game we know and love was officially launched in 1935. Of course, being the worldwide sensation that it is, certain editions are very collectable and there have always been special issues and tie-ins with film blockbusters such as *Star Wars*.

It is supremely ironic that one game turned up at the Farnborough Wind Tunnels show in 2012, linked with an extremely dubious money-related situation. This particular set – an exhibit from the Thames Valley Police Museum and part of the original evidence from the Great Train Robbery of 1963 – was brought to the show by the museum's curator. One of history's most infamous crimes, the Great Train Robbery took place on 8 August 1963 at Bridego Bridge in Ledburn, Buckinghamshire. With the help of inside information, the robbers rigged a signal and stopped the Glasgow to London mail train, stealing £2.5 million, equivalent to over £50 million today. The robbers did not have guns but they used coshes, severely injuring the train driver with a metal bar.

After the robbery, the criminals hid at Leatherslade Farm and killed time by playing *Monopoly*, apparently using real money. The police had calculated that they would stay within a certain radius and the robbers left the farm early before being caught in the dragnet. They paid an accomplice to burn down the farm in an attempt to destroy the evidence, but he failed to do so and the police discovered the *Monopoly* set which, by all accounts, yielded several sets of fingerprints. One of the gang, Ronnie Biggs, escaped from prison in 1965 after starting a thirty-year sentence. He lived 'on the run' for thirty-six years, gaining notoriety via a series of publicity stunts, including the recording of vocals for several songs released by the 1970s English punk band the Sex Pistols. He died in 2013.

So, '*would it be right to profit from crime?*' *Roadshow* specialist George Archdale thought not and valued the set at £100–200, although it will never actually be sold. In 2015, several items from the set came to light and were offered for auction. These included a 'Get Out of Jail Free' card, some houses and paper money from the original *Monopoly* set. They had been gifted by Ronnie to a friend and realised £400 at the sale.

# A THOMAS TELFORD
# GATE

Before each *Roadshow*, visitors can contact the office and ask for help in moving large items to the location for valuation or inclusion in the programme. This process has traditionally been known as the Furniture Round, although it is now called the Pre-show Pickups. Several specialists do this job, heading out for a few days before each show to meet and help as many people as possible.

In June 2015, miscellaneous specialist Marc Allum found himself doing the rounds on the Isle of Anglesey and mainland Snowdonia before the show, which was due to be held at the stunning setting of Plas Newydd, the home of the Marquess of Anglesey and the Paget family. Famously, Henry Paget, the first Marquess of Anglesey (and also known as the second Earl of Uxbridge), was second-in-command to the Duke of Wellington at the Battle of Waterloo, where his leg was almost blown off by a cannon ball. By all accounts he told Wellington, '*By God sir, I've lost my leg,*' to which the Duke apparently replied '*By God Sir, so you have*'.

The marquess' wooden leg is famously displayed in the house (now managed by the National Trust), which commands a spectacular position overlooking the Menai Straits, and linked to mainland Wales by Thomas Telford's spectacular Menai Suspension Bridge of 1819–26. Telford, one of Britain's finest civil engineers, was born in Scotland in 1757 and is responsible for some of the nation's greatest engineering achievements, including canals, harbours, countless bridges, aqueducts and roads. No one approaching the Island of Anglesey can fail to be impressed by this construction, still going strong almost two hundred years after its inauguration. It was originally gated for tolls and some of the original ironwork and gates associated with the bridge can still be viewed *in situ*. Nineteenth century photographs show the gates as intended by Telford and there is also one on display in the local museum.

After being contacted by an Anglesey farmer, Marc made his way to a rainy farmyard. Stood against the wall of a barn was what turned out to be one of the bridge's original wrought-iron gates. It was quite obviously correct, with its telltale radiating latticework pattern emanating from the corners. A pick-up was arranged and, on the day of the

*Roadshow*, Hilary Kay had the pleasure of meeting the gentleman who owned it, filming a lively and characterful piece. Hilary's valuation of £5,000–8,000 took the owner a little by surprise, but her estimation reflects the historical and financial importance of such an original finishing touch to Telford's bridge design. Quite fittingly, the piece about the gate was filmed within sight of the bridge.

# A YUAN BRONZE VASE

It is surprising how many *Roadshow* items – including the old, unusual and potentially valuable – have spent at least part of their life propping open doors. In 2010, *Antiques Roadshow* visited Victoria Hall, part of the Saltaire UNESCO World Heritage site in West Yorkshire. This famous model village was created around the large mill on the River Aire by the industrialist and philanthropist Sir Titus Salt, to house his mill workers and their families.

The busy show had already revealed some interesting items, including a large bronze vase that had arrived at Marc Allum's table. Having realised its significance, Marc lost no time in consulting oriental expert David Battie, who identified it as a Yuan Dynasty bronze. Established by the legendary Kublai Khan, the dynasty was officially in power from 1271–1368 and ruled as the first foreign lineage over the whole of China.

Naturally, David was extremely keen to film the vase and its provenance – including its one-time use as a doorstop – was quickly established. As the owner explained, his grandfather, who was a geologist, gold miner and meteorite hunter, had gifted it to him as a present for helping out with odd jobs. Apparently, Grandad had acquired it for just a few pounds during the 1970s from an auction house where it was used to prop open an office door. As David pointed out, the verdigris finish on the intricately decorated vase was consistent with burial in a grave. It also appeared that the base had been detached at one time, but later fixed back in place. At almost 60cm (2ft) high, the vase was certainly imposing and, as David suggested an estimate of £10,000–15,000 on camera, the owner was quite obviously shocked and pleasantly surprised to find that he had been given such an ancient and valuable item. At the time of writing, he still has the vase and there are no plans to sell it. His grandfather has now passed away, so the vase has acquired even greater sentimental value. However, for David it was the age that excited him. 'It is undoubtedly the oldest bronze we've featured on the *Roadshow*.'

# A BIZARRE
# FISHING ROD

For thousands of years, human beings have striven to enhance their lives by improving the design and practicality of everyday objects. Nowadays, every part of our lives – from space exploration to air travel, cars, cameras and kettles – is driven by technological advances, thanks to the efforts of myriad inventors, scientists, engineers and eccentrics. For all the ideas that work or are popular, there are many that never catch on or are sometimes downright bizarre. It would be true to say that many such items have surfaced on Antiques *Roadshow* over the years and none more so than a fishing rod that turned up at Hanbury Hall in 2015.

Those among us who are not fishermen should know that there are many technical aspects to the 'art'. Whether we are talking about fly-fishing on the Tweed, marlin fishing off the coast of Florida, or carp fishing in a local disused quarry pit, each has its own idiosyncrasies associated with bait and equipment. At Hanbury Hall, specialist Adam Schoon – whose passion for natural history, sporting and taxidermy material made him the man for the job – came across the oddest fishing rod that anyone had ever seen, and with an interesting tale to match.

The owner told Adam that the inventor of this bamboo rod was named John Henry Hirst. The rod measured 5.18m (17ft) long and was constructed like a modern crane with a 'spider web-like' support system to give it extra strength. When assembled it looked more like a giant pre-war radio aerial. Such a long rod has advantages – it has a much greater reach than others and Hirst was soon regarded as unbeatable in fishing competitions. He patented the rod in 1928,

but it was never commercially successful. The story does not end there, though. Private Hirst served in the First World War and used the rod to catch carp, eels and trout for fellow soldiers to eat. As he fished, the courageous Yorkshireman would regularly risk being shot at or killed by shells whizzing past him!

The current owner also brought along two bow-fronted cases containing stuffed carp that had been caught on the front line at Ypres. Both were annotated with an explanation and the date, having been prepared by a London taxidermist. Adam was intrigued by such an extraordinary tale of invention, courage and success – Hirst lived to fish another day, winning many fishing medals after the war. However, the rod remains the only one of its kind. Adam valued the rod and the cased fish at £10,000. With no plans to sell, the owner is undoubtedly proud to be the custodian of such a fascinating, unusual and museum-worthy object.

# A JAPONISME GEM

Specialist Eric Knowles knows a thing or two about antiques – especially decorative arts. At the Cleethorpes *Antiques Roadshow* in 1991, he was confronted by an exquisite jardinière manufactured by the French company, Christofle. The owner had inherited the piece from his parents who had purchased it in 1946 as one of several antiques, for which they paid £100. The owner's mother had a particular fondness for it.

The bronze urn and stand were gilded and patinated, the bowl decorated in cloisonné, an extremely intricate and complicated process involving the arrangement of 'cloisons' (small pieces of copper) to form a design, which are filled in with glass paste and fired. The piece then undergoes a time-consuming polishing process to reveal an intricate decorative finish that, in this case, portrayed cranes flying over tumultuous waves. It was indeed a craftsman's *tour de force* – for a European piece – in what is known as the Japonisme style.

As Eric filmed the piece, the owner recounted how his children had regularly used the jardinière as a goalpost because of its height – an event all too common among families who live with items rather than worrying about the potentially precious value of their possessions. The ensemble was engraved with the maker's motif, Christofle & Cie, and markings within the enamel on a shaped cartouche showed the date 1874. It had been shown at the famous Paris exhibition of 1889. A black and white photograph of the period shows it clearly on the corner of Christofle's stand. Emile Auguste Reiber became artistic director of Christofle in about 1870 and designed many items for the company. His work in the Japonisme style is regarded as the best of its type and he was undoubtedly one of the earliest and most influential exponents of the style.

Eric's appreciation of the piece was in absolutely no doubt and he valued it at £10,000. The astounded owner decided to put the jardinière back into the house and continue living with it, because his mother had loved it. Twenty years later he entered it for sale at a major London auction house, with an estimated price of £60,000–100,000, representing a considerable financial appreciation. Everybody was taken by surprise when the bidding climbed to an astronomical commission-inclusive £668,000!

As a footnote to the story, the owner was invited back to the Chenies Manor *Antiques Roadshow* in 2014, where he spoke about the meteoric rise in the value of the piece. As Eric Knowles

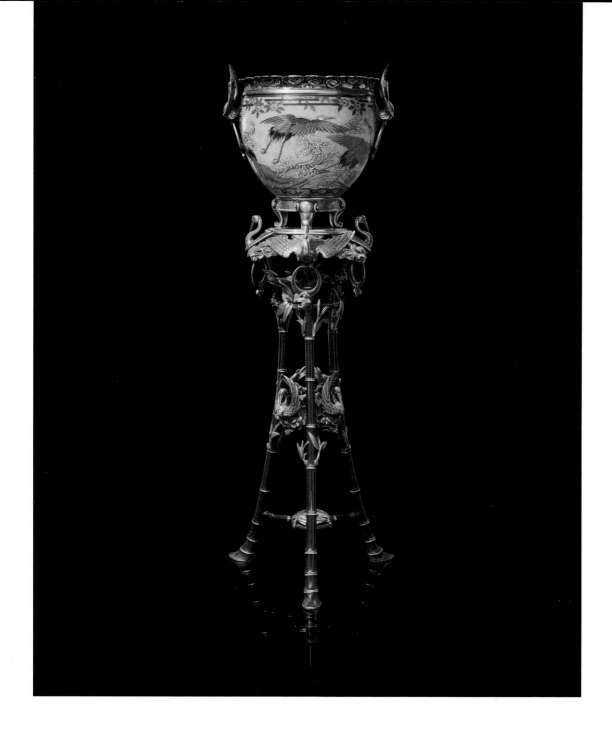

pointed out, the market had *'sprung out of nowhere'* — rising far beyond even the auctioneer's expectations. In effect, the owner had inadvertently made a wise decision to hang on to the jardinière and sell it at a more appreciative time. With great magnanimity, he had given much of the sale proceeds away to his family.

# A SUFFRAGETTE MEDAL

*'Georgina Healiss was my great-great aunt. I don't really know that much about her but we are all very proud of what she did and treasure her medal.'*

Liverpool's important, and sometimes turbulent, political history has surfaced from time to time during the *Roadshow*'s visits to that city. There have been several, with the most recent in 2007, and it was then that a lady brought in a suffragette hunger strike medal which had been awarded to her great-great-aunt in 1909. Over the years several such medals, and other objects with suffragette connections, have come to the *Roadshow*, and the families who have inherited them have always expressed their pride in telling the story behind the medal. For the experts involved, these medals have always represented both powerful emotions and a vital contact with an extraordinary chapter in our recent cultural history. In Liverpool the expert involved was Katherine Higgins who, as a woman, was particularly aware of the medal's potency and historical importance.

## GROUNDBREAKING ACTION

Any suffragette item on the *Roadshow* brings in the history of the WSPU, the Women's Social and Political Union. This was founded by Emmeline Pankhurst in Manchester in 1903 and became the driving force behind all suffragette activity until 1917, underlined by its famous motto, 'Deeds not Words'. Branches were set up all over Britain and, while the focus was inevitably on London as the seat of parliament, the movement was particularly strong in the north west, thanks in part to the long-established radical traditions associated with Manchester and Liverpool.

Georgina Healiss, one of five daughters of a boot and shoemaker from Stanley, joined the WSPU in 1906. Initially, she seems to have played a minor role in the expanding Liverpool branch, but in 1909 she appears in the records as a colour-bearer at the homecoming of Patricia Woodlock, following her release from Winson Green prison in Birmingham. The same year Georgina was arrested at a demonstration against the Prime Minister, Herbert Asquith, imprisoned and then released. She then took part in a demonstration in August 1909 against the visit of Lord Haldane, a government minister, to Sun Hall in Kensington, Liverpool, during which missiles were thrown. This event was fully reported in the 27 August edition of *Votes for Women*, the WSPU's newspaper. Georgina was arrested with six other women and taken to

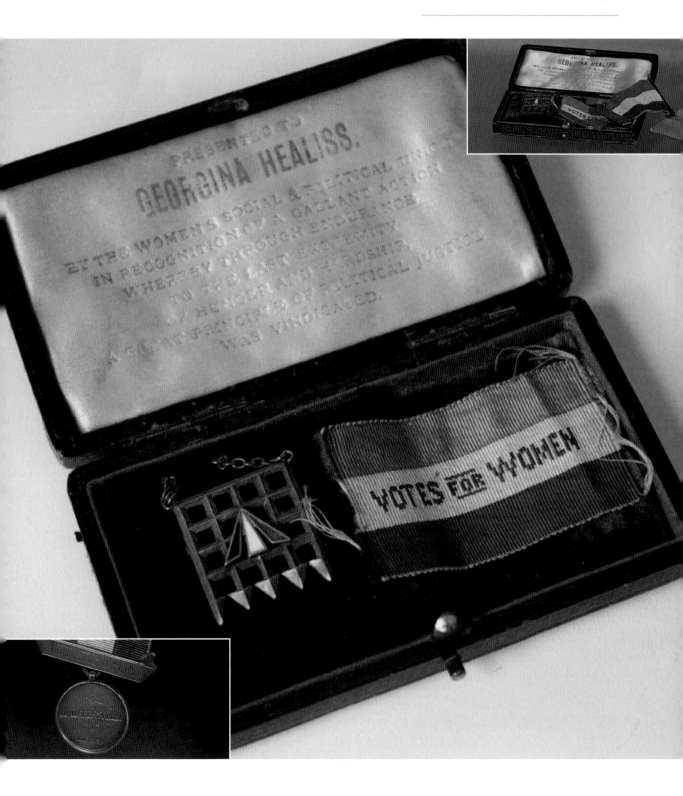

PRESENTED TO
GEORGINA HEALISS.
BY THE WOMEN'S SOCIAL & POLITICAL UNION
IN RECOGNITION OF A GALLANT ACTION
WHEREBY THROUGH ENDURANCE
TO THE LAST EXTREMITY
OF HUNGER AND HARDSHIP
A GREAT PRINCIPLE OF POLITICAL JUSTICE
WAS VINDICATED.

VOTES FOR WOMEN

Walton Goal, where they all went on hunger strike. She was sentenced to two months in prison but released the next day because of her critical condition as a result of the hunger strike. The other six women were released the next day for a similar reason, having not eaten for six days. For this, Georgina Healiss was awarded her hunger strike medal by the WSPU.

Introduced in 1909, these medals have become powerful symbols of the suffrage struggle and all it represents. The silver medal, with Hunger Strike on one side, and the recipient's name on the other, hangs from a ribbon in the WSPU colours and with a bar saying 'For Valour'. It came in a purple box with a personalised inscription.

## TIME IN PRISON

Georgina Healiss's mother was also a supporter of the suffragette cause, initially to help her daughter. However, she soon became more involved and in 1912 she took part in a window smashing raid in London, was arrested and sent to Holloway prison, but was soon released owing to her ill health.

The group of items brought to the *Roadshow* included Georgina Healiss's medal, with the original inscribed box, the portcullis brooch designed by Sylvia Pankhurst and given to every suffragette who had been sent to prison and a photograph of her. The brooch used the portcullis symbol of the House of Commons with an arrow taken from a prison uniform imposed on it. Katherine explained that the importance of the medal was that it was still with the family, and hoped that it would stay that way. She then valued the group at £10,000 to £15,000, a sum that clearly shocked the owner. A decade later this valuation seems rather reasonable, as WSPU hunger strike medals have since sold for over £20,000.

# A LINDNER PORTRAIT

The great appeal of the *Roadshow* to many of those who work on it is its total unpredictability. It is simply impossible to know in advance what each day will bring and so there are always plenty of surprises. Typical of these was picture expert Grant Ford's astonishment at finding a painting by an American artist of the Pop Art era at Trentham Gardens in Staffordshire in 2015.

Born in Germany in 1901 to an American mother and a German father, Richard Lindner started life as a concert pianist and then went to art school in Munich, before getting a job as an art director for a publishing company with strong Nazi connections. In 1933 he fled to Paris, worked as a commercial artist and was then interned in 1940. Subsequently, he served in both the French and British armies before fleeing to New York in 1941. Working again as a commercial artist and illustrator, he soon became part of that city's artistic community. In 1952 he started teaching at the Pratt Institute in Brooklyn and began to develop his distinctive style that brought together symbols of advertising, sexual imagery and strong colours, often reflective of gender roles in the media. By the early 1960s Lindner's style and imagery found a natural place in the Pop Art movement, and he met and worked with artists such as Andy Warhol. In 1967, Lindner moved to Yale University School of Art and Architecture, and the same year Peter Blake included him among the many people featured on the *Sgt Pepper* album cover, at the request of John Lennon. Lindner died in 1978.

When Grant asked the lady owner why she had the painting, she revealed that Richard Lindner had been her uncle – her father's brother. She went on: '*The last time I saw him was in 1968, he got off the train all in denim and smoking a little clay pipe. He was just a great person to have in the house.*'

Grant replied that the painting, a vibrant watercolour of the composer Offenbach, surrounded by a swirling mass of figures and images, was one of the most extraordinary and unexpected things he had ever seen on the *Roadshow*. Clearly signed and dated 'Paris, 1935', the painting belonged to an earlier period of Lindner's life and showed the influence of artists such as Chagall, Klee and Kandinsky, well before he developed in New York the style for which he is now famous. Yet, it seemed at the same time to anticipate the Pop Art movement. For that reason, Grant valued the painting for £40,000 to £60,000. The owner said that it would be kept in the family for sentimental reasons and be passed on to her sons and grandsons.

# FIJI BULIBULI CLUB

*'It's one of those things that happen to other people on the* Roadshow. *You never really think it will happen to you.'*

*Roadshow* experts in the miscellaneous section are regularly shown tribal and ethnographical items, but the majority are inevitably tourist pieces brought back from visits to Africa, Australasia, Southeast Asia or the Far East. These may, of course, have some age, reflecting the emergence of the popular market for tribal souvenirs from the early years of the twentieth century. Much rarer are original, high-quality tribal artefacts brought back to Europe by explorers, missionaries and others during the nineteenth century. With such pieces, provenance is very important, for they are generally hard to date without some kind of documentary evidence.

## THE IMPORTANCE OF PROVENANCE

This was the first question asked by miscellaneous expert and tribal art enthusiast Ronnie Archer-Morgan when confronted by a Polynesian club brought in to the Scarborough *Roadshow* in 2012 in a black bin bag. The lady owner told him it had belonged to her grandfather, a solicitor in Scarborough, to whom it had been given many years before by two elderly Scottish spinster clients. These ladies may have been connected to the extensive Scottish community living and working in the South Pacific in the nineteenth century, but there was no evidence to confirm this. The first governor of Fiji in 1875 was a Scot, Sir Arthur Gordon, and he is known to have given Fijian artefacts to friends and relatives, a typical route for tribal things to come back to Britain.

Ronnie explained that the club was a bulibuli, a war club from Fiji, and that it certainly dated from the ninteenth century, or was even late eighteenth century. He explained that, while Polynesian war clubs came in many forms and styles, this one with its graduated spherical head and intricately patterned shaft was typically Fijian. He then said: '*It is a magnificent club, the best I have seen, and the quality of the carving and the size — it is over a metre long — tells me that it was made as a prestigious object and a status symbol for a chief. It is far more than just a war club, it is an unbelievable object.*' For this reason he valued it for £30,000 to £35,000, making it one of the highlights of the Scarborough programme when it was transmitted.

The owner and her family were amazed, not expecting the club to have any real value. As they explained later: '*We had always liked it. It's beautifully carved and very interesting to look at but we had no idea it would be valuable. We just wanted to find out more about it.*'

## TO SELL OR NOT TO SELL?

In due course, the family decided to sell the club. Naturally, the *Antiques Roadshow* cannot give specific advice about selling objects, nor can the experts be involved in any way with the owners after the event. This is essential in protecting both the privacy and security of the owners and the integrity of the programme. *Roadshow* valuations are usually based on auction prices and, in many cases, the experts make this clear when they give a valuation.

Some, on the other hand, give the equivalent of a value that would be put on the object by a top antique dealer. In high street terms, these two valuations represent wholesale and retail prices, and the difference between them can be very considerable. In the case of the club, Ronnie gave the latter – the retail valuation.

When tested in the market place, the owners settled for a lower amount.

# THE TORY LOO SEAT

It would be pointless to hold a competition to find the most unusual object to have come to a *Roadshow* because there would be so many entries. However, those that make the short list would probably all be chosen because they bring together the bizarre and the historical in an unusual way.

The annual conferences of Britain's main political parties have, over the decades, been held in cities all over Britain. For years, Blackpool was a favourite, particularly with the Conservatives, with notable speeches over the decades, from Winston Churchill in 1954 and from Norman Tebbit in 1981 when he suggested that the unemployed should '*get on their bikes.*' It was when the *Roadshow* visited that famous Lancashire resort that an extraordinary witness to political history was brought in by its lady owner, in the shape of a wooden lavatory seat. She explained to Judith Miller that it had originally come from the former Conservative Club on Blackpool's Victoria Street, where it had been installed in 1899. She went on: '*When the conference ended, it was like a stampede, as they all rushed to the club to use the loo.*' After a period in use in another club, the lavatory seat had been abandoned in the cellar, from where the current owner had rescued it. Apparently, the party Chairman had tripped over it and told her to get rid of it, so she had taken it home, with his permission. She said: '*I didn't even have a bag, I just walked home through the streets with it under my arm.*' The seat is inscribed '*In memory of those who sat here.*' Judith and the owner then discussed the many famous names that might have used it, including Winston Churchill, perhaps with a cigar. The owner felt that it should have had a visitors' book attached to it.

For Judith, it was a classic example of an object that, while having no financial value, was an important part of history. She said: '*It brings together novelty, entertainment and great history. I think it is fabulous.*'

After the programme was transmitted, the story aroused considerable interest, and some local Blackpool Conservatives even suggested that they should have the seat back. However, the owner is determined to hang onto it.

# A DOLLS' HOUSE

*'When I saw the house itself, I was almost speechless.'*                    Fergus Gambon

The *Roadshow*'s visit to Tewkesbury in 2016 was typically enjoyable, with a lovely setting by the abbey, a sunny day and a big crowd. However, the day was made remarkable by two exceptional and extremely unusual items, an eighteenth century painted silk dress, and some very early dolls.

Many *Roadshow* team members have enthusiasms and knowledge outside their normal area of specialisation, and for ceramics expert Fergus Gambon, it is dolls' houses and early dolls. So, he was very excited to be dragged away from the long ceramics queue to look at a group of

dolls. He had seen early dolls before, notably at Swindon, where he valued one for £20,000, but these turned out to be far better than he had expected. Firstly, they were a group and seemed to represent a family, with both males and females featured. Secondly, they were very early – probably dating from the first decade of the eighteenth century. Thirdly, they were in excellent original condition. Dolls of this type, often made from wood by specialist craftsmen, and sometimes known collectively as Queen Anne dolls, were popular in Britain between the 1680s and the mid-eighteenth century. For Fergus, this was an extraordinary find and he explained how the dolls were made individual by their painted expressions and their clothing. He was also pleased to see that they were accompanied by some pieces of furniture and a miniature stump work embroidered box of the same period.

The owner then revealed that there were more dolls at home, along with the house in which they lived. He explained that they had always been in the family, handed down from generation to generation from 1705, when they were made for a lady named Elizabeth Westbrook. He had not been able to bring the dolls' house to the *Roadshow* as it was large and extremely delicate but, from the description, Fergus knew he had to see it. So, after a discussion with the production

team and the owner, it was agreed that they would break all the *Roadshow* rules and send Fergus with a camera team to the owner's house, to film the dolls' house *in situ*. This was duly done and so in the finished programme Fergus was able to talk about the dolls, and their house.

## EVOLUTION OF THE DOLLS' HOUSE

The earliest dolls' houses – generally known as baby houses – took the form of a cupboard or box with shelves, in which the dolls and their furniture were displayed. The doors were plain, without any details hinting at architecture or domestic housing. The importance of this one is that it is the earliest known with an architectural façade, a tradition previously thought to have developed later in the first half of the eighteenth century. Early architectural examples include famous houses in Stranger's Hall, Norwich, Nostell Priory and Uppark House, and it is these that are normally credited with the start of the tradition that has determined the look of dolls' houses to the present day.

This house also dates from a period from which very little has survived, and is made even more important by its clear provenance and direct line of descent from 1705. Fergus said: '*When I saw the items from the house brought along by the owner, I was awe-struck. And when I saw the house itself, I was almost speechless. I think I must have made a very subdued recording! There is something remarkable about an undisturbed early baby house. The rooms and contents that I was seeing had been viewed by eighteenth century eyes, and I expect they smelled the same unique smell that each house has. Once these houses leave the family or are split up, they lose their magic.*'

At the time, the owner did not seem to share Fergus's excitement, and admitted he had never opened it before. However, when Fergus told him that it was a dolls' house of national importance and worth £150,000 to £200,000, he looked at it with new eyes.

# AN APOTHECARY CABINET

On a hot summer's day in June 2011, the *Roadshow* visited Lulworth Castle in west Dorset. Over 3,000 people turned up, bringing the usual variety of treasures, curiosities and things from the attic. However, one of the best things seen that day – an eighteenth century apothecary's cabinet – did not have to travel far, as it lived in the castle.

The cabinet had a rather chequered history. Although the actual origins were not known in detail, it had been associated with the castle and the castle's owners for a long time – or at least until 1929, when a disputed will left by a soldier killed in the First World War caused many of the chattels in the castle to be removed from Lulworth, including this cabinet. Soon after, a fire destroyed Lulworth Castle and most of its surviving contents. A year later, the cabinet appeared in a local auction and the family were able to buy it back, along with other pieces that had been removed under the terms of the will.

Lennox Cato examined the cabinet, which at first sight appeared to be a pedestal desk, in great depth, pointing out the details of its design and manufacture and its 421 oak-lined drawers. He explained that its use as an apothecary's cabinet made it a great rarity among surviving English furniture of the mid-eighteenth century. In the discussion with the owner, Lennox attributed the piece to William Hallett.

Although an important name among eighteenth century cabinet makers, Hallett's life is a bit of a mystery. Born in Somerset in about 1707, he seems to have been an upholsterer, auctioneer and frame maker as well as a cabinet maker. His workshop was in Great Newport Street, in the heart of London's eighteenth century furniture trade. By the 1750s, he had made enough money to buy himself a country estate, build a house and have his portrait painted by Francis Hayman. Hallett left much of his estate to his grandson – also William Hallett – who with his wife is the subject of Gainsborough's famous double portrait, *The Morning Walk*, painted in 1785. Few fully authenticated pieces of furniture by Hallett are known, and Lennox admitted that, without original accounts or other documentary evidence, he could only attribute it to Hallett.

Nonetheless, Lennox was still prepared to value the cabinet for £200,000.

# A SHAKESPEARE NOTEBOOK

*'Sometimes the best things come in small packages.'*  Matthew Haley

Nothing brings the past to life as directly as a handwritten manuscript, for these can represent a unique and personal link to the period when they were written. The most obvious and regularly seen are letters and diaries, generally not written with publication in mind, by both famous people and by others long forgotten. More unusual are documents connected with historical events, drafts and notes relating to books and scripts for plays, films and television or radio programmes, and over the years the *Roadshow*'s book experts have seen some unusual examples of these.

## A QUESTION OF IDENTITY

One of the best appeared at the Caversham *Roadshow* in 2016 in the form of a small commonplace book, or notebook, densely filled with what appeared to be seventeenth century handwriting. Matthew Haley saw at once how important it could be, for he was able to establish quickly that all the notes were about Shakespeare and included quotes from his plays, sometimes identified by name. He explained that anything that related to Shakespeare and was written either during or soon after his lifetime was hugely important, offering both insights into his life and times and, more importantly, contemporary comments about his plays. Such matters are of great interest to the current generation of Shakespeare scholars, who are intrigued by how Shakespeare's plays were received at the time they were originally written. In his *Roadshow* recording, Matthew could do no more than glance at the notebook and pick out a few entries, but he made it clear that further research was bound to uncover much more about the notebook's contents and possibly even reveal the identity of the writer.

## FAMILY MATTERS

For the owner, there was a direct family connection. '*My five times great-grandfather was John Loveday of Caversham Court and he was a great antiquarian and traveller who amassed a library of around 2,500 books and manuscripts. I suspect that this notebook came down the family from him but I can't be certain. It just appeared with my mother's belongings and I'd never seen it before.*'

When the Caversham *Roadshow* was transmitted, there was immediate interest in the notebook, and so the owner lent it to the Bodleian Library in Oxford in order that a transcript

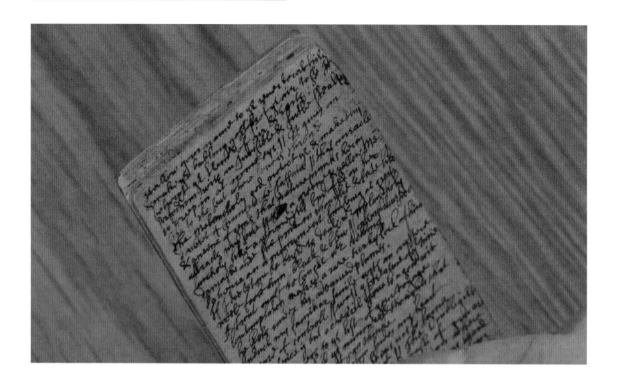

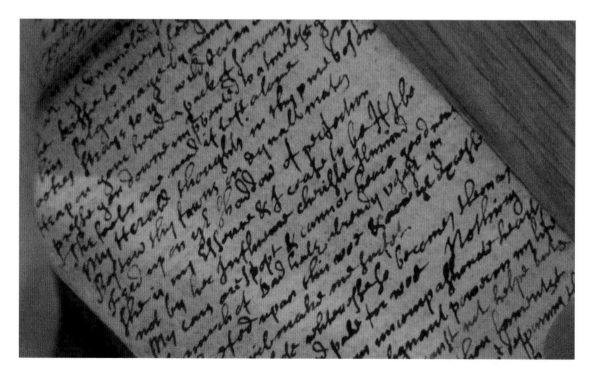

could be made, and further research carried out, in the hope that some of the questions it raised could be answered. These include who wrote it, what did they have to say and why did they write it? It could also establish whether the writer was actually connected to the owner's family. Even more intriguing is the question about when it was written, and whether this was close to Shakespeare's lifetime or later, perhaps during the Puritannical Cromwellian period, when plays and theatre-going were frowned upon.

## THE MYSTERY CONTINUES

In due course the notebook may reveal its secrets, but even in the short exposure it had on the *Roadshow*, the excitement it generated was palpable, both at the time and subsequently. For Matthew, and for the *Roadshow*, it was a major discovery, possibly unequalled during the programme's forty years. At the start of the recording Matthew said: '*Sometimes the best things come in small packages*.' At the end, he valued the commonplace book for £30,000, while adding that detailed research into the content and history could greatly increase that value.

# BANKSY LOVERS

*'Within twelve months we would have been closed.'*                    Youth club manager

As many of our viewers know, *Antiques Roadshow* is a Bristol-based programme, broadcast from the famous BBC building on Whiteladies Road. As a result, it has a certain loyalty to the city and over the years has featured several interesting Bristol locations, notably Ashton Court in 2014. The ancestral home of the Smyth family, Ashton Court is famous for its Humphrey Repton-designed grounds and 850-acre deer park, all within a stone's throw of Isambard Kingdom Brunel's famous Clifton Suspension Bridge.

On that day in 2014, a steady stream of visitors braved the equally steady drizzle as the scene was set for a story that later made headlines around the world. It centred around 'Mobile Lovers', a piece by Banksy, the enigmatic Bristol-born artist who shot to fame with his distinctive street art and graffiti, born out of the Bristol underground scene. His characteristic stencilling can be found on walls in public places and on private buildings in Bristol, London, Brighton and elsewhere around the world. His darkly satirical, incognito hit-and-run approach to art has made him both notorious and highly collectable, his work often changing hands for hundreds of thousands of pounds.

## ART OR GRAFFITI?

Despite Banksy's work being featured in legitimate exhibitions worldwide, graffiti remains technically illegal in Britain and many people see him as a vandal. Councils have removed his work in various locations (although not Bristol), because they do not wish to be seen to condone graffiti.

Controversially, some of Banksy's work – including his image of the Grim Reaper in a boat (an allusion to the 'Great Thames Stink' in nineteenth century London) on the side of a former cargo ship in the Bristol docks – has sparked ownership disputes.

Appearing on a section of wood in a doorway of Bristol's Broad Plain Boys' Club – actually attended by Banksy years ago – 'Mobile Lovers' is another example of 'ownerless art'. The picture depicts a couple locked in an embrace but checking their mobile phones over each other's shoulders. It was brought to the show by the youth club owner, who told a very excited expert, Rupert Maas, the story of how it simply appeared in their 'doorway'. The club later

removed it because they feared that it would be stolen, but it did spark an ownership dispute between the club and Bristol City Council. Rupert valued the work at £400,000.

## BROAD PLAIN BOYS' CLUB

Already 120 years old, Broad Plain Boys' Club was experiencing financial difficulties and in danger of closing. During the ownership dispute, Banksy sent a letter to the youth club confirming 'Mobile Lovers' as one of his works and donating it to the club. This was just the kind of philanthropic gesture that the club needed and 750,000 people came to see the piece on display in Bristol City Art Gallery and Museum.

The work was sold to a private collector for £403,000, which gave the youth club the lifeline it so desperately needed. Some of the money benefited other youth organisations in the voluntary sector. To show their gratitude to Banksy, and as a tribute to his internationally acclaimed style, the youth club exhibited their own street art 'thank you' in the form of a large graffiti panel.

# AN ENGLISH ROSE KITCHEN

The venue was the Sainsbury Centre at the University of East Anglia, in 2013. The stunning setting of architect Norman Foster's high-tech building – with its world-class museum – made a wonderful backdrop for the day's items. This futuristic edifice was one of Foster's first major commissions, designed between 1974 and 1976, and houses the collection of Sir Robert and Lady Lisa Sainsbury, begun in 1930s and amassed throughout their lives. In 1973, they very generously donated the collection to the university. It now numbers several thousand objects, including major sculptural works, paintings and antiquities, housed in a purpose-built area – The Sainsbury Centre.

This was a wonderful location for the *Roadshow* team, who were lucky enough to be let loose among the collection the night before with staff and curators – always a privileged experience. The arrival of a kitchen was also an unusual experience in *Roadshow* history. For expert Marc Allum, it was also an opportunity to talk about something that we might ordinarily take for granted – the humble kitchen sink. It's a cliché, but Marc could not resist using it as the owner described why he had brought a kitchen to the show. The story was that he had bought a house, taken a dislike to the kitchen – traditionally named 'English Rose' – removed it and put it in the garage! In fact, the striking cream and red modular design of this 1950s kitchen was groundbreaking rather than traditional. Manufactured by Constant Speed Airscrew Industries in Warwick, the English Rose kitchen had evolved out of the wartime aircraft industry. The company had made parts for Spitfires and Lancaster bombers. As production ceased after the Second World War, they found themselves with empty order books and a great deal of surplus aircraft-grade metal. Their innovative answer was the English Rose kitchen, now heralded as a post-war classic and very popular with retro enthusiasts. Valuing the kitchen at £1,000, Marc explained how aircraft design had influenced both the look and construction of the kitchen with elements also borrowed from American kitchen design. Even at the time, the price of the kitchen was far beyond the pockets of ordinary people. According to the price list, a single wall cupboard cost an eye-watering £9 at a time when the average weekly wage was £8. Clearly loath to part with it, the owner had even moved house, taking it with him to yet another garage.

A while later, the kitchen appeared on a well-known internet site and did indeed sell for the figure suggested by Marc. It was eventually – and very deservedly – installed in a new home.

*Now installed in a new home, the kitchen comes back to life.*

# JFK'S FLYING JACKET

Great names in history regularly feature on the *Antiques Roadshow*. The show at Kent's Walmer Castle in 2015 was no exception – a fascinating array of items topped off by a letter signed by the Duke of Wellington, a past owner of Walmer Castle. Nothing, however, had prepared expert Jon Baddeley for the arrival of a leather jacket belonging to the 35th President of the United States, John F. Kennedy, better known as JFK.

Few people have made such an impact on the psyche of an entire nation than this popular, glamorous, All-American war hero, whose colourful life and illustrious career were tragically cut short by assassination on 22 November 1963. That moment in American history will forever be engrained upon a generation that remembers, with horror and sadness, the images of poor Jacqueline Kennedy scrambling across the open-topped limousine. There have since been many conspiracy theories surrounding this media-friendly, seemingly family-oriented president, whose numerous extra-marital conquests included the actress Marilyn Monroe. These were kept well hidden from public view, no doubt thanks to the efforts of his close and trusted coterie and good relationships with the media.

One such liaison that has come to light took place with Gunilla von Post, a young Swedish aristocrat. The depth of JFK's feelings for this woman was confirmed by the sale, in 2010, of several love letters written by him to her. The pair met on the Cote d'Azur in 1953, when Gunilla was just twenty-one and JFK, then a thirty-six-year-old senator, was just three weeks away from marrying Jacqueline Bouvier. Two years later Gunilla and Kennedy spent a week together. JFK left his leather jacket behind, and sixty years later this same jacket turned up at Walmer Castle.

Provenance is everything with such items. The owner's father had been given the jacket by Gunilla's family. The size 44 jacket would indeed have fitted the then senator, and the story seemed watertight. So what could it possibly be worth now? Given the strength of interest in items associated with JFK and the 2013 sale of a bomber jacket for a staggering $570,000, Jon was confident about valuing the jacket at £250,000. He said, '*The story's everything, please write it down. I feel confident the market will pay that price. In America or anywhere – worldwide – it is an iconic piece.*'

We all hope that the jacket will be offered for sale in the not-too-distant future.

# ROMMEL'S CIGARETTE PACKET

*'I opened the door and there, standing behind the desk, was Field Marshall Rommel, so I gave him the courtesy of standing to attention.'*

The old, traditional notion of the stiff upper lip in the face of adversity is one that will always be associated with the British. As far as *Antiques Roadshow* is concerned, the best example was Welshman, Mr Roy Wooldridge. At the grand old age of ninety-five, Mr Wooldridge came to the Tredegar House show in 2014 and told militaria expert Graham Lay an extraordinary tale about his exploits during the Second World War, using photographs, a scrapbook and his medals.

Within the scrapbook was a black and white photograph, annotated in large letters '*Monty and Me*', showing Mr Wooldridge being presented with his first Military Cross (one of two awarded to him during the Second World War) by Field Marshall Montgomery. In a lively and humorous manner, he recounted a most extraordinary brush with death while searching for German mines on

the French beaches, just before D-Day. As a newly promoted (and married) captain, he had been ordered away from his wife of just three days on a highly dangerous night-time mission to help clear the beaches (later, D-Day landing sites) of German mines before the arrival of allied troops. The task required him to be dressed in plain clothes. If caught by the Germans, this would immediately designate him as a spy and ensure his execution by firing squad.

## A MEMORABLE EVENT

Unfortunately, Captain Wooldridge's dinghy was sighted by a German U-boat and he and a colleague were captured. After being repeatedly interrogated and threatened with being handed over to the Gestapo, the hated and feared German secret police who would have almost certainly executed him, he was blindfolded and taken to a French château, where he was marched up a flight of stairs.

By this time, the *Roadshow* crowd was hanging on Roy's every word, captivated by this astonishing tale of courage. To everyone's surprise, Roy revealed that the room at the top of the stairs was occupied by no less than General Erwin Rommel, arguably the most respected

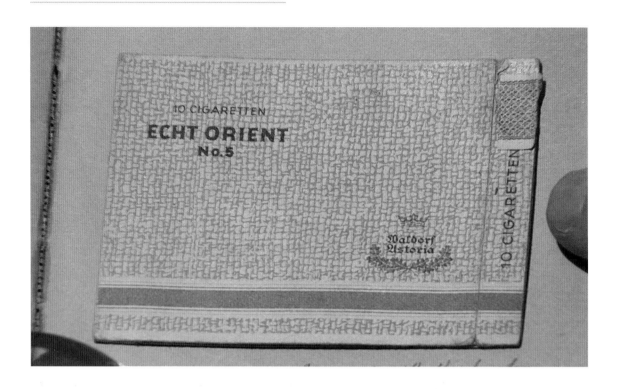

of all wartime German officers, both among his own and the allied troops. His reputation as a brilliant strategist and soldier who eventually opposed the criminal ideology of the Nazis is the stuff of legend. Roy Wooldridge related how he had given Rommel '*the courtesy of standing to attention*'. He said, '*I respected him as a clean fighter; under his command there were no atrocities by the German troops*'.

## BRAVERY REWARDED

Under questioning by Rommel, Roy divulged only his name, rank and serial number, and Rommel asked if there was anything that he wanted. To the delight of the *Roadshow* audience, Roy answered: '*I'd like a pint of beer, a packet of cigarettes and a good meal please.*' The general could have had him shot as a spy but, instead, Roy was taken to the mess, presented with a stein of beer, some cigarettes and a hearty meal. He was later escorted to a prison camp in northern Germany, where he spent the last years of the war. On the table, in the scrapbook in front of Roy, was the empty German cigarette packet.

Both Graham Lay and the audience were very moved by Roy's self-effacing and engaging account. Graham valued his amazing collection of medals and artefacts at £10,000. However, nobody was surprised when Roy replied with a hearty '*Not for sale!*', provoking further laughter from the audience. Roy later appeared on a Christmas special but, sadly, both he and Graham Lay have since passed away. Roy's family donated his Military Cross to the Imperial War museum and, in time, the other items may find their way there, too. His appearance will forever be a very memorable and moving *Roadshow* moment.

# OLD TESTAMENT FIGURES

*Antiques Roadshow* has ventured abroad on several occasions, but its first overseas trip took place in 1989, when it visited Kronborg Castle near Elsinore, north of Copenhagen in Denmark. Made famous by its association with Shakespeare's *Hamlet*, the castle is regarded as one of the finest in Europe. It was here that Lars Tharp and David Battie stumbled across some mysterious Old Testament figures.

Unusually for Bible figures, these four were Chinese in origin, made of cloisonné enamel and annotated with Chinese text. Common within Chinese art, this lengthy, labour-intensive process involves the intricate application of copper cloisons to the formed base, be it a vase or figure. These cloisons are then in-filled with glass powder suspended in a paste, fired and then polished. Measuring an average twelve or thirteen centimetres in height, the four figures depicted Moses, David and both young and old Isaiah. This intriguing juxtaposition between Christian ideology and Chinese beliefs caused an interesting debate between Lars and David as to how old the figures might actually be. Lars thought that they were eighteenth century, but David suggested the nineteenth. As it was getting late in the day, they asked the owner if he could attend the next *Roadshow* venue – Malmö in Sweden – a couple of days later, and he obligingly agreed.

In the meantime, Lars and David debated the potential origin of these immensely rare figures – a photograph of their encounter appeared in the national newspapers. What the owner had to say simply added to the mystery. The figures had been given to his father by a family of Italian Jews as a 'thank you' for helping them escape from Italy to Switzerland, either just before or during the Second World War. Since then, they had apparently languished in his father's barn in New Zealand.

Lars valued the figures at between £8,000 and £12,000. They were later put up for sale at Sotheby's and sold for around £9,000 to a New York dealer, who apparently sold them on to a private collector. Some years later, they were gifted to the Metropolitan Museum of Art in New York, where further explanations were offered as to their provenance. The figures could indeed date from the eighteenth century and were most likely made for a Jesuit or Jewish client by Chinese craftsmen, possibly forming part of a clock group or cabinet decoration.

Their original route to Europe is unknown but they subsequently found their way to London as loan exhibits within the Victoria & Albert Museum's 2004 exhibition *Encounters: The Meeting of Asia and Europe 1500–1800*. The figures are now permanently housed in the Metropolitan Museum of Art in New York.

# JEAN DUPAS POSTERS

In 2009 the *Roadshow* visited Stanway House in Gloucestershire. This classic Jacobean Cotswolds manor, with its Arts & Crafts Movement associations, was the unlikely setting for the discovery of some iconic work by one of the major French designers of the Art Deco era.

Jean Dupas, who was born in Bordeaux in 1882, was a noted painter, designer and graphic artist whose work spanned Art Nouveau and Art Deco. During his long life, his output included drawings for fashion magazines, painting, frescoes and murals, interiors for major ocean liners – notably the *Ile-de-France* and the *Normandie* – and a large variety of graphic art, including posters and catalogues. While most of his work was for French clients, Dupas also produced a famous set of posters for London Transport, commissioned by Frank Pick. Today, Dupas is for collectors one of the top French Art Deco artists, and so many later copies and reproductions of his work have been produced.

Therefore, when Judith Miller was shown a group of Dupas posters, she was stunned to find that she was looking at originals, and not the copies she expected. In conversation the owner then revealed an extraordinary story. In the early 1970s when he was eleven, he was, as he put it, '*dragged*' to an auction by his mother. Thoroughly bored, he wandered round the saleroom on his own, and then found under a table a pile of old posters. Randomly looking through them he saw that some of them featured images of trains and ships and so told his mother he wanted them. His mother told him to bid and he offered 50p, which was all he had but this proved to be enough and they went home with 102 posters. At home, his initial excitement soon waned, and they were put away and forgotten, to be rediscovered much later. At this point he looked at them properly and found that the collection included some of the great names of the 1920s and 1930s, such as McKnight Kauffer. Some were then framed and hung in the hallway of his house. Wanting to know more, he brought a selection to the *Roadshow*.

Among these were four great posters by Jean Dupas, and it was these that excited Judith. She explained that the first print runs were small and so original examples in good condition were rare, and highly desirable and then astonished the owner by telling him that each of the four Dupas posters was worth £10,000. She ended by saying, '*I wonder what else you've got at home in your 50p lot.*'

# A CHINESE ARMORIAL DISH

The beautiful Tywi valley, in Carmarthenshire, Wales, was the setting for the 2009 season's Welsh show at the historic Aberglasney House and Gardens. The rare Elizabethan promenade garden is said to be the best surviving example of its kind in the British Isles.

Asian specialist John Axford was working his table as usual when a lady presented him with a supermarket carrier bag. The bag contained a large porcelain plate or charger, almost 56cm (22in) in diameter and decorated with a large armorial. John explained that the plate represented the arms of the Hohenzollern family and that it had been commissioned by the Royal Prussian Asiatic Company for Frederick II of Prussia (1740–1786), the longest-reigning Hohenzollern monarch. Frederick the Great, as he was known, was a great moderniser and is credited with turning Prussia into one of Europe's strongest military powers, particularly following a highly successful Seven Years War (1756–63). History also depicts Frederick as a 'glorious warrior', so the interest in his dynasty and the objects associated with it is therefore high. The provenance of the plate was a little vague, but the family had married into German lineage at some point and it is thought to have originated in Germany.

Made from hard paste porcelain, the plate had been crafted in China around 1750–1755 and was part of an extensive service. Custom-decorated, personalised Chinese porcelain was hugely expensive and ordered by the rich and the aristocratic as a symbol of wealth and status. In some cases, clients waited years for their services to arrive, only to find out (when they were finally delivered) that the Chinese makers had misunderstood the instructions, either miscopying details of the design or annotating the ceramics with words from the descriptions.

The story of Frederick's service is less than straightforward, as well – apparently, a large part of the luxurious ceramics cargo was lost when the ship carrying it, the *Prinz von Preussen*, ran aground on an island in East Fresia. Some pieces of the service have come up for sale over the decades, but most are displayed in major museums. As John pointed out, previous values have reached tens of thousands of pounds and he did not hesitate to estimate the worth of this particular plate at a staggering £80,000 – the highest value ever placed on a piece of ceramic on *Antiques Roadshow*. The plate was later privately sold, to a foreign royal family for around £60,000. Quite a sum for an article brought along at the last minute as an afterthought.

# A FRODSHAM
# MANTEL CLOCK

Expert Richard Price always has the time for a fine clock. They are his specialist area and he has seem some superlative examples of clocks, watches and timepieces in the many years of his tenure on the show. This was certainly the case on the show's visit to the gloriously colourful and famous gardens of the picturesque Tudor mansion, Chenies Manor House, in Buckinghamshire.

When *Roadshow* specialists use phrases such as '*finest*', '*best I've ever seen*' and '*I'll never see another like it*', you know that the valuation is likely to be on the high side. The obvious quality of an important object automatically shines on HD screens and the Sunday evening armchair game of guessing the value echoes around the living rooms of the United Kingdom as the expert builds the tension. In this case, Richard was able to pull out all the stops. The piece in question was an undeniably pretty rosewood mantel clock signed Arnold, Charles Frodsham, 84 Strand, London, 1825.

If there is a name in the clock world that excites people, it is Frodsham. Born in 1810, Charles Frodsham heralded from a family of clock and watchmakers and was apprenticed at a young age. He was to become one of the most eminent horologists of the nineteenth century. The Frodsham reputation for producing precision timekeeping instruments was global. Having purchased the already renowned company of John Roger Arnold, he moved into their premises on the Strand in London, in 1844 and cemented a reputation that was to make him the favourite of royalty and scientific institutions. His chronometers and regulators won medals the world over and he also became 'Superintendent and Keeper of her Majesty's Clocks at Buckingham Palace', an obviously prestigious appointment. His business also carried the Royal Warrant.

As you can imagine, Richard was naturally very taken with this clock and began to describe it to the owner. Clock talk can be very technical and the jargon somewhat incomprehensible to the layman, but Richard was in his element as he described the obvious lack of pendulum but truly portable platform lever escapement and top grade double fusée movement. As the icing on the cake, it also transpired that the clock had apparently been given to its original owner – a lady-in-waiting – by Queen Victoria, who frequently patronised Frodsham. Although the lady's name was lost to history, Richard pointed out that it was typical of Victoria to order such quality items to give to people that were close to her. The clock itself – numbered 825 – sits nicely in a timeline of Frodsham productions. It was also very fine, incorporating several features such as exceptional engraving and a beautifully pierced and engraved gilt 'mask' around

the dial. As Richard described it '*the finest English clockwork*'. Viewers were in no doubt that big numbers were going to be involved and the estimate of £30,000 seemed wholly justifiable for such a beautifully made and historic clock. After the show, the owner decided to sell the clock and it eventually went to auction with a major London saleroom, where it showcased in a Fine Clocks sale and sold for £34,000. The story was followed up for the 2014 Christmas special.

# A CARTIER WRIST WATCH

In 2011, *Antiques Roadshow* visited the imposing neo-classical mansion of Castle Coole. Designed by the famous English architect James Wyatt, the house sits in a 1,200-acre wooded estate in Enniskillen, County Fermanagh, Northern Ireland, and was built between 1789–1798, for the 1st Earl Belmore. As at most *Roadshow* events, the jewellery table experts were working apace to keep up with the queues for one of the show's most popular subjects. Sometimes an object turns up which is undermined by its poor appearance and tatty condition; however, the experts are well accustomed to seeing through this initially poor impression and are adept at looking for clues that can ultimately mean it is something a little more special. This was the case with a wristwatch presented to John Benjamin.

As the story unfolded on camera, the owner explained how the watch had been given to a great uncle and had subsequently been consigned to a garage, where it had resided for some thirty years, unloved and in non-working condition. John cleverly enthused about the light and shade of the watch, balancing the fact that the poor condition would heavily affect its value whilst ultimately revealing that it was in fact a rare Cartier watch. Founded in Paris in 1847 by Louis-François Cartier, this famous jewellery brand became known the world over for its fabulous creations. To the amazement of the owner, John then valued the watch at £5,000. However, that was not to be the end of the story.

Behind the scenes, the idea of a restoration was mooted and the watch was eventually sent off to the Cartier workshops in Switzerland. The model, an early Cartier 'Tank' with its distinctive cabochon winder, was dated to 1924 and made in Paris. The restoration carried out by Cartier's top craftsmen included a restored dial, new hands and a replacement winding stem. When the watch came back to the show at Hillsborough Castle in 2014, John and the owner were able to discuss the incredible restoration. The transformation was truly amazing and so too was the value. The world of wristwatch collecting has in recent years become more intense than ever, with an increasingly popular reputation for investors and collectors. John mooted a value of around £40,000 – but the only real measure of such a rarity would be to offer it for sale. In this instance, the family have decided to hold on to the watch. Nevertheless, they enjoyed the journey of seeing it restored to its former glory, as did many *Roadshow* viewers.

# MRS AMBROSE'S PUNCH POT

What would you consider to be a life-changing windfall? In this day and age, in which lottery prizes routinely amount to tens of millions of pounds, there is an expectation that a win has to be very big indeed to enable someone to 'get on' in life. However, the value of a win can also be relative, and this was illustrated beautifully by the story of a lady named Nora Ambrose.

The year was 1989, the location Liverpool and the object a rather large green and mottle-glazed ceramic 'teapot'. The owner, a Mrs Ambrose, had joined the queue with the apparent expectation of being turned away because her item was cracked and chipped. She eventually found herself in the company of expert David Battie and – innocently and unwittingly – on the way to *Antiques Roadshow* fame. Mrs Ambrose explained that the 'teapot' had always been used as such by the family until it was wrapped up in an old tea towel and retired to the top of the wardrobe. As David explained on camera, the 'teapot' was, in fact, a punch pot made in the mid-eighteenth century and known as Whieldon ware. Made of creamware and coloured overall with a mottled green, yellow and brown glaze, the body of the pot was decorated in concentric lines and its spout was in the form of a stylised snake. It was originally developed by the famous Staffordshire potter, Thomas Whieldon, a one-time partner of Josiah Wedgwood. Having become very popular, this style of pottery was frequently copied by other Staffordshire potteries, making it very difficult to attribute many specific examples to Thomas. However, David was delighted by the piece and decided to tease the owner about what it might be worth. At first, he suggested an estimated value of £150, gradually building up the suspense until he arrived at a final valuation of £5,000–£6,000, leaving her completely flabbergasted. The pot was subsequently entered for sale with a major London auction room, where it achieved a dizzying £14,300.

For Nora Ambrose, this was a life-changing amount of money. From the proceeds of the sale, she was able to purchase her council house. Sadly, after many subsequent *Roadshow* visits, she is no longer with us, but the story remains a classic, standout *Roadshow* moment.

# MARTINWARE
# COLLECTION

*'Love, loathing and plain curiosity.'*                                                    Will Farmer

Some locations provide a superb combination of high-value items with a stonkingly good story, too. After all, one of the show's tag lines is *'What story will you bring?'*, emblazoned in three-foot high letters on the side of the huge *Roadshow* pantechnicon as it travels to venues around the country. It is fair to say that Walmer Castle, in 2015, provided especially rich pickings, in terms of excellent stories and interesting, high-value objects – including some intriguing but ugly pottery made by four brothers.

The old adage *'beauty is in the eye of the beholder'* really does ring true in the art world. Martinware is a case in point – like Marmite, you either love it or hate it. Yet Martinware has a fascinating history of innovation, providing a bridge between the aesthetic of the Victorian age and the advent of modern studio pottery.

Founded by Robert Wallace Martin in 1873, the Fulham-based pottery specialised in saltglaze stoneware. Robert and his three brothers, Walter, Charles and Edwin, each took on different areas of responsibility within the production and management of the business. Their distinctive output ranges from thrown pots to pieces sculpted by Robert, appropriately entitled 'Wally birds'. Often known as 'tobacco' jars, these extremely characterful pieces have detachable heads that are renowned for their all-seeing expressions. They were often caricatures of well-known personalities of the time, making each one absolutely unique.

## AN ACQUIRED TASTE?

Expert Will Farmer has a particular interest in this field and was therefore delighted to see several pieces of Martinware at the show. The owner explained that many years earlier he had been left a very small Martin brothers vase. This inspired an interest and he continued to pick up such items at auctions throughout the comparatively inexpensive 1970s. As Will pointed out, the fact that such pieces were being sold at auction indicated an appreciation for their work, although the pottery was still very much derided. Will buffed up the owner's ego a little by referring to him as *'a pioneer, out there at the front'* for his foresight in buying early on. Will played the 'ugly' card too, but as most appreciators of Martinware know, the beauty is exemplified in that very ugliness. When asked what he had paid for a particular double Wally bird, the owner

replied that it had cost £450 in 1976, which roughly equates to about £3,500 in today's values.

The large single bird had cost £650. These are not inconsiderable amounts of money for the time. There was also a vase and other, smaller pieces on the table, as well. Will focused on a firing fault on the beak of the main bird – which was dated 1884. After talking down the acceptability of damage to serious collectors, he then promptly valued the piece at a huge £40,000. Both the owner and the audience were incredulous.

Dated slightly later, at 1907, the double bird was similarly talked down by Will because of its lesser stature. However, he then valued this item at a whopping £60,000, accompanied by further gasps of incredulity from the audience. Their reaction, and the owner's words, 'it's unbelievable', capped off a great story.

These high values are testament to the appreciation now afforded to Martinware, an area of the market that has rocketed in recent years. Good examples of the Martin brothers' work routinely achieve well in excess of these amounts. For the owner, his collection proved to be a good investment, but for Will it was a simply magical *Roadshow* moment.

# LLOYD'S PATRIOTIC FUND SWORD

In 1688, according to Lloyd's Register, a gentleman named Edward Lloyd opened a coffee shop in London's Tower Street. The appropriately named Lloyd's Coffee House was frequented by ship-owners and sailors and soon became a meeting-place to discuss trade and maritime matters. The dealing that took place there eventually led to the establishment of the insurance market – Lloyd's of London and Lloyd's Register. On 28 July 1803, a meeting was convened and the decision taken to establish a patriotic fund. Its initial purpose was to give grants to those wounded in action, help the dependants of those killed in the service of the Crown and make awards to servicemen who went above and beyond the call of duty. Such was the outpouring of generosity that, in less than a year after the fund was established, donations totalled £179,000.

The awards included money, beautifully decorated dress swords or silverware, such as the Patriotic Fund Vases designed by the eighteenth century British sculptor and draughtsman, John Flaxman. The dress swords were issued in different 'denominations' – £30, £50 and £100. The most valuable were generally given to commanders or naval captains. Most famously, twenty-three £100 swords were issued to captains who took part in the Battle of Trafalgar under Nelson's command.

In 1985, the *Roadshow* was visiting Ipswich, when veteran militaria expert Roy Butler spied a tell-tale gilt lion's head protruding from a plastic bag. As it turned out, it was a Patriotic Fund sword, which more than fulfilled his expectation that the bag held something really special. Although it was late in the day, a recording spot was made available and Roy was delighted to talk about the history of the Patriotic Fund and its swords. This example – a £100 sword – would have been used as a ceremonial or full dress accoutrement, but never for battle. Roy valued the sword at a substantial £8,000, although the current estimate might easily be around £20,000–30,000. Over many decades, the Lloyd's Patriotic Fund gained a reputation for generosity and the ability to raise morale. It still does exemplary work among armed forces-related individuals and with charities.

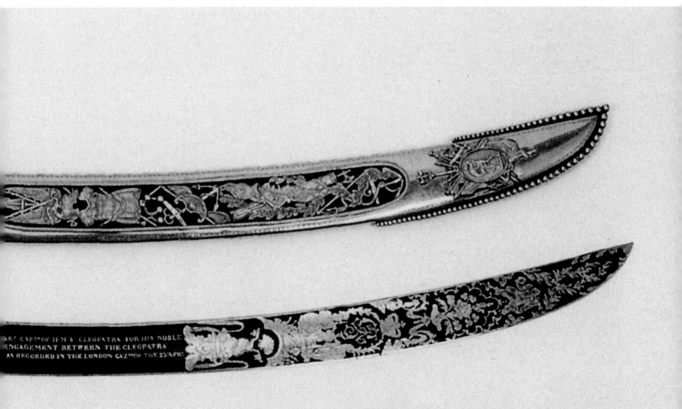

# CROMWELL'S FUNERAL FLAG

*'An object which is almost radioactive with power.'*                                        Hilary Kay

Belton House in Lincolnshire is often cited as an example of a quintessentially English country house. Built in the 1680s, its simple, elegant symmetry served as a stylish backdrop for the show held on a beautiful summer's day in July 2014. This was when expert Hilary Kay came face-to-face with an object of huge historical significance that initially proved extremely difficult to value.

The object in question was a painted coat of arms belonging to none other than Oliver Cromwell, arguably one of the most controversial figures in British history. An MP and powerful military commander during the English Civil War (1642–1651), Cromwell fought successfully on the side of Parliament against the Royalists led by King Charles I. After the Royalist defeat his was one of fifty-nine signatures on the captive king's death warrant. After Charles' execution in 1649, Parliament established the Commonwealth, ruling the British Isles as a republic. Four years later, Cromwell took power as Lord Protector of England, but he died in 1658 of what historians now think was a severe urinary infection. Cromwell's son Richard ruled briefly afterwards but failed to secure the all-important support of the army. His resignation paved the way for the restoration of the monarchy and the accession of King Charles II in 1660.

## A SINGULAR ITEM

The owner explained that her father had acquired the piece, together with a collection of militaria, and it had been kept in the spare room. As founder members of the English Civil War Society (a famous battle re-enactment group), her parents had a great affection for the item and wanted other people to see it. Interestingly, the 'standard' also bore an inscription suggesting that it had been taken by a young boy from the 'hearse' carrying Cromwell's body to his grand burial in Westminster Abbey.

The owner described the standard as *'one of those objects that makes you tingle'*. Hilary agreed, saying it was *'one of the trickiest things I've ever had to value'* and she made a very intelligent stab at £25,000.

Determined not to let it rest there, Hilary followed up the story on an episode of *Priceless Antiques Roadshow*, with very interesting results. Given the pomp and ceremony surrounding the funeral, It turned out that the 'standard', a hand-painted 'escutcheon' (emblem bearing a

coat of arms) was one of many lining the processional route and/or decorating the interiors of Westminster Abbey and Somerset House (where the Lord Protector lay in state). This begged the questions – had the item really been taken from the hearse, and was it at all real? A useful starting point was a visit to the Museum of London, where another example of the 'Scutcheon' (archaic English for escutcheon) survives. Even more tantalising was the earlier sale, at a major London auction house, of another example bearing a similar inscription, albeit in far, far worse condition. This had realized £4,000, no doubt because of its fragility and damage. Further investigation led to Westminster School were it was confirmed – on camera – that an '*escutcheon bearing a Latin inscription had indeed been taken by a Westminster Schoolboy from the coffin, and it was still preserved in the school library!*' This was perhaps slightly disappointing for the owner, but it did confirm that the story was true, although someone had fraudulently embellished some original surviving examples of the remaining standards from Cromwell's funeral, probably during the eighteenth century. The mystery was finally solved. Not only was the standard real and had been present at Cromwell's funeral, but it was not the one stolen from the hearse.

## A GRISLY END

As a footnote, following the restoration of the monarchy, Cromwell's body was exhumed and ritually 'executed' at Tyburn, along with several other dead or living regicides (signatories to King Charles' death warrant). His body was decapitated and the head stuck on a pole outside Westminster Hall for nearly twenty-five years. The head is apparently buried under Sidney Sussex College in Cambridge, but the exact whereabouts are unknown.

# JANE AUSTEN'S CUP-AND-BALL

While 'Bilbocatch' may sound like something out of J.R.R. Tolkien's *The Hobbit*, it is actually a game – more commonly known as 'cup-and-ball'. It also happened to be a favourite pastime of Jane Austen, the famous English novelist and author of *Pride and Prejudice*. Apparently, she was so adept at landing the ivory ball on its turned post that she could easily achieve this over one hundred times in succession.

In 2008, expert Paul Viney was asked to assess some Jane Austen-related material at the Exmouth show. One of the objects was an ivory cup-and-ball game that, it transpired, was still owned by the direct descendants of Jane Austen. Suffice to say, the very idea of holding an item that had been so close to such an important historical figure was very exciting indeed. The name 'bilbocatch' is an Anglicism of the French name for the game '*bilboquet*', popular during the late eighteenth and early nineteenth centuries. In a letter to her sister Cassandra, dated 29 October 1809, Jane Austen makes a clear reference to the game: '*We do not want amusement: bilbocatch, at which George is indefatigable; spillikins, paper ships, riddles, conundrums, and cards, with watching the flow and ebb of the river, and now and then a stroll out, keep us well employed; and we mean to avail ourselves of our kind papa's consideration, by not returning to Winchester till quite the evening of Wednesday.*'

As was typical of such items during the Georgian era, Jane's cup-and-ball was made from turned ivory. Her game consists of an ivory ball drilled with a hole and linked by a string to the turned handle or post. The idea is to flick the ball onto the slightly dished 'cup' at one end, or on to the slightly tapered point by means of the hole in the ball at the other. This should be simple enough, you may think, but it is actually far more difficult to do than it looks! Different versions of the game can be found in various parts of the world, including one named '*Kendama*' in Japan.

Jane Austen's game was not an easy item to value but, having come down through five generations of the family, its provenance was certainly in no doubt. Paul thought it was worth £20,000–25,000. The family eventually decided to sell, entering the game for auction at a major London saleroom in 2016, with an estimate of £20,000–30,000. However, the game did not sell, and is now on display at Jane Austen's House Museum in Hampshire. Interestingly, a letter from Jane to Cassandra, which was estimated at £40,000–60,000, made a staggering £150,000 in the same sale.

# THE CRAWLEY SILVER

'The Crawley Silver' sounds rather like some long-lost, fabled treasure worthy of a Hollywood script which, in a way, it was. For Ian Pickford, one of the *Roadshow*'s long-time silver specialists, the arrival of a young man and his mother, plus several carrier bags, at the Crawley show in 1993 presaged a find to beat all finds.

The young man in question was dressed in a highly individual way with a hairstyle to match. Of course, that should not make any difference to how a person is treated, but his unusual appearance was definitely at odds with the stereotypical image of a collector of good antique silver. The story was that during the 1960s and 1970s, his father (now deceased) secretly collected pieces of early silver. He kept these hidden from his wife, who did not share his interest. The family did not have much money to spare at the time and, looking back, the man's passion probably made a difference to the household finances. It was only after his death that his wife and his son and daughter discovered the pieces – and their original receipts – carefully secreted around the house.

It soon became apparent that the plastic bags held some incredible rarities, including a Commonwealth tankard and a beautiful Victorian stag's head stirrup cup, which Ian valued at £10,000. There was also a silver box inlaid with a piece of the famous Boscobel Oak in which Charles II hid after being defeated by the Parliamentary army at the Battle of Worcester in 1651. Ian put a total value of over £200,000 on the items that he saw that day, pronouncing it as '*the very best collection*' he had ever seen at a *Roadshow*.

The following year, twenty pieces sold at auction for £78,000. One of the star lots was a James I parcel gilt wine bowl bearing the date 1607. Thought to be unique, this piece realised £13,000 and was later resold in London for £28,750. Although the family has retained a few items as keepsakes, others have been auctioned off over the years, finding buyers both in the United Kingdom and abroad. By all accounts, the final tally has been nearer to £350,000 – an incredible amount for objects kept for many years in shoeboxes under the bed!

# A GEORGE
# RICHMOND
# MINIATURE

*Antiques Roadshow* has been to the Channel Islands several times. In 1995, it visited Jersey's capital St Helier, where something of a record relating to the size of a picture was achieved. The painting in question – an enigmatic miniature on ivory by George Richmond, measuring just over 21 x 14 cm (8 x 5½in) – was assessed by expert Peter Nahum. Perhaps better known for such works as the portrait of author Charlotte Brontë (hanging in the National Portrait Gallery), Richmond went on to achieve fame as a great portraitist, mainly working in chalk and crayon. Initially, however, the nineteenth-century painter was part of small group of artists based in Shoreham, Kent. They called themselves 'The Ancients' and were ardent admirers of William Blake, the great poet and artist, whom Richmond had met at the age of sixteen. Like other writers, artists and musicians of the time, the group sought to portray an idealised and romantic view of the simple pastoral life.

The exquisite picture confronting Peter was an early work entitled *In the First Garden*, painted by Richmond at the age of nineteen in 1828. Blake's influence was more than obvious in both composition and style. Shortly afterwards, the painter eloped with his wife-to-be, Julia Tatham, to Gretna Green, where they were married in 1831. Together they had fifteen children, ten of whom survived. Richmond's work as a portraitist provided a bread-and-butter living to support the family, although he ultimately became very sought after. The painter died in 1896 and is buried in Highgate cemetery.

This particular picture had passed down through the family via the artist's daughter. In 1897, it had been offered for sale in London, but she bought it back for what was then the huge sum of £210. Peter Nahum enthusiastically extolled Richmond's great talent, emphasising the importance of the small picture which, when sold the year after the show at a London auction house, realised £63,250. This made it the most expensive 'value relative to surface area' object seen on the *Roadshow* – up to that point!

# A CARAVAN PLANNED
# BY A P.O.W.

*'He had to do something to keep his sanity.'* Graham Lay

Poignant stories abound on the *Roadshow* and many are closely related to the heroic wartime exploits of soldiers, their families and the sad aftermath surrounding war and all its horrors. Tales of bravery and endurance are not rare, yet they touch our sense of humanity every time. One such story came to light in 2013 at Gregynog Hall in Powys (Wales), home to the famous Davies sisters, whose philanthropy established the house as a centre for the arts and which now houses the art collection that they left to the nation.

Graham Lay, the show's militaria expert, got off to a good start that morning with the arrival of a small, rather ragged-looking book covered in brown paper. Unprepossessing items frequently turn out to be the most interesting and, in this instance, the small book contained

284

something quite miraculous. It had belonged to the owner's father, an officer who had been taken prisoner by the Japanese in Borneo during the Second World War and held for three and a half years. Being an officer, he was required to do very little, which was both a blessing and a curse. The officers were so bereft of any entertainment or mental diversion that they invented ways to occupy themselves. In this case, the owner's father started to draw up plans for a caravan. Apparently, he had no previous experience of either owning or designing one, so the colourful illustrations and very precise measurements and notes were all derived from his imagination, as were the costings. Looking forward to better days and, perhaps, constructing it for himself on his return after the war, was something that obviously gave him purpose and kept him going. The book itself was made from parts of envelopes and salvaged paper. Prisoners were not allowed such items, so they posted lookouts to make sure that no-one would be discovered while using pencils and paper. At the beginning of his interment, the owner's father weighed 102kg (16 stone); on his release he was barely 44kg (7 stone).

## A UNIQUE DESIGN

Entitled a 'Lightweight – two-berth trailer caravan', it was typical of designs of the period, quite streamlined in a 1930s sort of way with all mod cons, including a sink and water system and leaded glass windows. Every fitting, latch, window hinge, handle and structural detail had been carefully designed and explained, and it seemed as if the plans would make a perfectly good caravan. The total cost of the project came to £45 and 18 shillings.

After his return at the end of the war, the owner's father married almost immediately. His daughter explained that he never talked about his experiences in the camp – a very common story amongst people who have endured such hardships. Perhaps his expectations to build the caravan were superseded by his new life and love. Sadly, he died young, at just fifty-three years of age. Graham put a notional value on the book but, of course, it was priceless to the family.

## SEEING THE LIGHT OF DAY

In 2014, sometime after the book's appearance on the show, the family were contacted by an independent television production company that mooted the idea of building the caravan. Famous for their *Amazing Spaces* programme, George Clarke and Will Hardie took on the challenge. The result was amazing: although a few design changes had to be made, these were relatively minor, considering that the plans had all been born out of a POW's imagination. The show kindly donated the caravan to the family and the sheer joy involved in seeing his plans finally realised was a fitting testament to a man who, like so many, had endured so much.

# 'MAY THE FORCE'

Merchandising is something that we are all used to these days. Every blockbuster film that is released, every franchise, comic book or video game generally tends to have something commercial associated with it. Items can range from action figures to pencil rubbers, duvet covers to breakfast bowls; in our modern, consumer-driven society, the marketing opportunities are endless. However, 'movie' merchandising is nothing new. Disney has always exploited this market – how many people have owned a Mickey Mouse watch? Other famous stars in film history have also been represented in the same way – Charlie Chaplin, for example. However, none of these examples quite prepare you for the phenomenon that is the movie franchise *Star Wars*, for which creator George Lucas took merchandising to another level.

Rather like an urban myth, the tales of Lucas becoming a billionaire from the merchandising of his films alone are part of modern folklore. It seems that, since 1977, no child has wanted to be without a lightsabre or a Princess Leia action figure. The same applies to many adults, for that matter. *Star Wars* merchandising is a business beyond comprehension and the collectors' market is huge.

For collectables specialist Mark Hill, encounters with such fans of the genre are frequent on the show. At Bolsover Castle in 2015, Mark was able to wax lyrical about a good-looking display of material brought in by an ardent fan. The collecting of *Star Wars* items – like most things related to film, comics and television – has a lot to do with nostalgia – which is also very much age-related. This contributor had been collecting since before the release of *Return of the Jedi*, the third film in the original trilogy, which dates from 1983. Most of his collection was boxed, which is an important factor for collectors; in fact, some empty *Star Wars* boxes can sell for thousands of pounds alone. In 2016, a rare figure of Boba Fett, the notorious bounty hunter, sold for £26,000. Alas, Mark's man did not have anything quite that valuable, although like many collectors he confessed that his collection had sat under dust sheets in the loft for the last ten years. Mark placed a value on the collection at around £700–900 and the owner was pleased. Not long afterwards, his toys were consigned to auction, where they made a healthy £1,100. No doubt, like many other collectable genres, *Star Wars* memorabilia will continue to capture the imagination of many generations to come and values will continue to rise.

# AN L. S. LOWRY PAINTING

While working the tables at an *Antiques Roadshow*, it is normal for an expert to be overwhelmed by the length of the queues and a constant stream of valuations. The sheer hard work is all part of the job, of course, but sometimes there is absolutely no way that someone on one side of a venue can know that something amazing might be happening at the other. It is not uncommon, therefore, for specialists to hear only at the end of the day that a real treasure has passed through that they did not even get a glimpse of.

This was not the case at a show held in Oldham in 1999. The 'bush telegraph' quickly went into overdrive to alert other specialists to the presence of a painting by Laurence Stephen Lowry. The lucky expert charged with the hands-on experience of filming the piece was Stephen Somerville. The owner was a gentleman whose wife had been a friend of Lowry's and had chauffeur-driven him after he had retired. So far so good!

Lowry was born in Stretford in Lancashire in 1887. There is a tendency to call him a naïve artist, suggesting that he was untrained and that he merely happened upon painting as a pastime. This is simply not true. Lowry studied at the Manchester school of Art under the tutelage of the French Impressionist Pierre Adolphe Valette, and later at the Royal Technical Institute in Salford. However, his 'day job' – as a rent collector for Pall Mall Property Services – continued until he retired on his sixty-fifth birthday in 1952.

Lowry's famous style is particularly distinctive. His '*matchstick men and matchstick cats and dogs*' have almost become a cliché, but his stark rendition of northern industrial landscapes and streetscapes, with their tonal distinctiveness and weather-less skies, historically set the tone for a career that blossomed into worldwide acclaim for his individual perspective and observations on life.

Dated 1937, this particular canvas had never been exhibited, and the painter would have been fifty years old when he finished it. Still relatively unknown at this point, Lowry's success was bolstered by an exhibition at London's Lefevre Gallery later in 1939, but the additional presence of a cigarette packet, drawn on and signed by Lowry and also brought to the show by the owner, further reinforced the story. His wife had apparently persuaded Lowry not to toss it out of the car window! Given the massive increase in the value of Lowry's work, there are many fakes and copies in existence and Stephen was keen to emphasise this painting's impeccable provenance. At the time, he valued the picture at £100,000, a figure that would

now be surpassed many times over. Some of Lowry's pictures have since sold for millions of pounds. By all accounts, the owner was sent home with a security guard – something that does not often happen on *Antiques Roadshow*.

The vast majority of the painter's works – a collection of over 300 pieces – are housed at The Lowry, a purpose-built gallery on Salford Quays. He may have an international reputation but Lowry's ethos shines through in his comments on his own painting:

*'I am not an artist, I am a man who paints'*.

# BULL'S HEAD
# STIRRUP CUPS

Some *Roadshows* are particularly memorable because the experts get to stay on site. Where this is possible (and permitted), it can be a great pleasure to roll out of bed in the morning and get straight to work. In 2010, the team descended to sample the delights of the castellated, early fifteenth century Hampton Court Estate in Herefordshire. Owned by the same family since 1510, the estate was purchased during the early nineteenth century by John Arkwright, the son of the famous eighteenth century industrialist Richard Arkwright, also known as 'the father of the modern industrial factory system'.

John Arkwright was certainly wealthy enough to run the huge estate. As many of the *Roadshow* specialists who stayed there in 2010 will confirm, the corridors filled with armour and grand furniture may not have been original to the house, but they certainly bore witness to its enduring grandeur. When silver expert Alastair Dickinson was presented with a group of silver stirrup cups, he explained that stirrups have no feet, so therefore cannot stand up, and were used only for a quick 'slug' before riders went off on a fox hunt. As a result, most cups take the form of foxes' or stags' heads. Unusually, one of the cups shown to Alastair was in the form of a bull's head and bore the mark of Hunt and Roskell, founded by the famous English silversmith Paul Storr in 1819 and later jewellers and silversmiths to Queen Victoria.

As Alastair pointed out, bulls' heads are one of the rarer forms of stirrup cup. The lady talking to Alastair (the owner) explained that the cup had been commissioned by the castle owner, John Arkwright. It bore a hallmark for 1869, placing it at the time when Arkwright was raising his medal-winning Hereford cattle – very much a symbol of agriculture in the county – on his 10,500-acre estate. With their distinctive red coats, this breed produces prime beef cattle and is now world famous. At the time, Arkwright was also winning prizes at such major agricultural events as the famous Royal Show in Warwickshire. Every time one of his cattle won a prize, he had a stirrup cup commissioned in its likeness. We know for a fact that there were at least twelve winners, because there was a set of twelve stirrup cups! Alastair appeared a little casual about the valuation when he said '*There's not going to be much change left out of £150,000*', but he was truly amazed at being confronted with an unbelievably rare and valuable set of silver stirrup cups. By the way, these cups did, in fact, stand up – after a fashion – because the horns and the noses on the bulls formed a perfect tripod, giving them extra stability!

# DICKIN MEDALS

Militaria expert Graham Lay dealt with a whole range of gallantry and service medals in the course of his long career with the *Antiques Roadshow*. Yet, how many of us were aware that medals were also given to animals that proved helpful in times of conflict? At the Stowe show in 2012, it was fascinating to see a collection of five Dickin medals that had all been awarded to pigeons. Known as the Victoria Cross of the animal world, the award was instituted in 1943 by Maria Dickin, the founder of the People's Dispensary for Sick Animals (PDSA). A total of fifty-four bronze medals were awarded between 1943 and 1949, thirty-two of the recipients being pigeons.

The five medals were brought to Stowe by the general manager of the Royal Pigeon Racing Association (RPRA). He professed himself keen for people to have knowledge of them, rather than leave them hanging on the walls of his office. Quite alarmingly, when filming began Graham read out a German pamphlet, issued as a warning during the Second World War, about a Frenchman executed for releasing a pigeon, obviously to send information to the Allies. Incredibly, a quarter of a million homing pigeons served during the war. They were sent out with every bomber crew and, in case of a crash or radio loss, could be used to send a message home with intelligence or the co-ordinates of the stranded airmen. The pigeons were parachuted to the likes of the French Resistance and would find their way home, dodging the guns of German marksmen who were stationed on the shores specifically to shoot them down. The National Pigeon Service had designated numbers for each serving bird. One of the awards mentioned by Graham was for pigeon NPS42, which made three trips back to Britain with messages. The pigeons may have saved thousands of lives and their role cannot be underestimated.

When asked, the RPRA's general manager admitted that the medals were insured for £9,000. On hearing this, Graham thought long and hard, pursed his lips and voiced his own insurance estimate – a hefty £180,000–200,000!

After the show, interest in the medals was huge and they were exhibited at the Imperial War Museum. In 2000, the Dickin medal was revived and has been awarded fourteen times, retrospectively and to recognise new courageous animals.

# A LEWIS CARROLL COLLECTION

Most people have never heard of Charles Lutwidge Dodgson but mention the 'White Rabbit' or the 'Cheshire Cat' and people immediately recognise them as characters from *Alice in Wonderland*, one of the world's most popular and famous works of literary fiction. Born in 1832, Charles Dodgson is far better known as Lewis Carroll, his pen name. He was an intelligent man, gaining a first-class honours degree in mathematics at Oxford. He had other talents, too. His (mainly satirical) writing had been published and he was also a very good photographer, so much so that he is often referred to as a writer, mathematician and photographer. The idea of *Alice's Adventures in Wonderland* (the full title of the work) apparently came to Carroll in 1862. In part, it was based on a young girl named Alice Liddell, one of the daughters of the Dean of Christ Church College, with whom Charles had become great friends. By all accounts, he had related the tale of Alice to the young Liddell girl while on a boat trip and she persuaded him to write it down. The rest, as they say, is history.

The sequel, *Through the Looking Glass, and What Alice Found There*, followed in 1871. Charles initially illustrated the original manuscripts himself, but the drawings in the published versions were produced by the famous Victorian artist John Tenniel. Lewis Carroll's characters have provided us with some of the most popular cultural references in the literary world. Although his works are actually classified as children's books, most people agree that many of the underlying references and themes are, in fact, very adult indeed.

In the antiques world, anything to do with Lewis Carroll has become incredibly sought after. Books and manuscripts expert Clive Farahar became part of that story in 1994, when the *Roadshow* visited Blenheim Palace. A gentleman, whose aunt named Annie Rogers had apparently known Carroll, brought along several signed first editions with a direct connection to the author. There was even a letter to the aunt herself from Carroll. This initial visit – which was interesting enough in itself – was followed by another encounter three years later at Christ Church College, where Carroll himself had studied. Amazingly, the owner had returned with even more material including letters, photographs by Carroll and presentation copies of his books signed in his characteristic lilac-coloured ink. Among the pristine titles there were some early foreign translations in German, Dutch and French. '*It was the sheer quantity and quality of the collection that was astounding,*' Clive said.

*Alice's Adventures in Wonderland* was much beloved by Queen Victoria, as well as countless other readers down the years. For generation after generation it has been reworked and re-imagined, yet it almost always holds true to the initial concept of those famous Tenniel line drawings. Clive valued the collection at £150,000, but who knows what it might be worth now.

# AN INDIAN PORTRAIT

The appreciation of art is very subjective – beauty is very much in the eye of the beholder. When a bold portrait appeared at the imposing venue of Arley Hall, Cheshire, in 2016, there was certainly a mixed response to the style of the picture. Expert Amin Jaffa opened with a line that few paintings' specialists would have disagreed with – '*you might think you're looking at a portrait by a European artist of the 1930s*' – and indeed, the vivid, striking and heavy impasto portrait certainly looked of that period. However, it bore both a signature and a definite date of 1954. As the owner explained, it was actually a picture of his mother and had been painted in India. The owner's father had worked for Grindlays Bank – an institution with a heritage stretching back to the 1820s – and the artist, named Krishen Khanna, was a young employee with the company. He had lodged with the family for a while and a relationship had thus grown out of this association, and as a struggling artist he had painted the portrait. Khanna subsequently went on to become one of India's twentieth century greats, and Amin found himself looking at one of his earliest works.

Khanna left the bank in 1961 to become a professional artist – a brave step to take for someone who was essentially self-taught. As Amin explained, Khanna's place in Indian art is important. He is regarded as one the great modern painters of India and has achieved global status, as well. His style, rooted in European painting of the 1930s, has since won him several prestigious awards. His popularity is also an interesting illustration of how Indian culture has progressed and embraced new styles of art.

With increased wealth, fuelled by the burgeoning economy, the nature of collecting has changed and Indian art collectors have come to love their own home-grown artists. As a result, they are also keen to buy back and collect earlier works, of which this was a good example. The increased global popularity of artists such as Khanna is in part due to the mobile nature of Indian entrepreneurs, their internationally based businesses and their desire to collect. Amin was obviously pleased to explain to the owner the importance of such works in the twentieth century timeline of Indian artists. He did not ponder over the valuation for very long and came through with an extremely robust £30,000–50,000. This drew a slightly shocked '*crikey*' from the owner, which was little wonder really, as the painting might easily have been dismissed by some as an amateur work.

# AN EARLY DOLL

In 2008, the *Roadshow* set up for business at STEAM, the Museum of the Great Western Railway in Swindon, Wiltshire. This amazing-looking venue certainly provided an eye-catching set for the show, despite a few technical hitches. Halfway through the day, a little treasure appeared in the form of a very old doll, carved in wood and dressed in yellow silk. The owner explained that she had been aged around eight when her aunt had given her the doll and, it transpired, the doll had previously passed through many generations of the same family.

Although rather shabby and worn-looking, it was obvious that this was no ordinary doll. The owner's family believed that it had been modelled on Queen Victoria's mother, Princess Victoria of Saxe-Coburg-Saalfeld, Duchess of Kent and Strathearn. However, as Fergus pointed out, the dress was not of the correct fashion for that period; the fact that the doll's yellow silk dress was supported underneath by a pannier placed her in an earlier period.

Like many dolls, she would have been of great personal value to the child for whom she was made. This rather aristocratic-looking doll was clearly not the plaything of a poor youngster. With a gesso-covered and painted face, glass eyes, real human hair, articulated limbs and intricately embroidered dress – albeit now faded and frayed – she utterly captivated Fergus. After careful consideration, he dated her from around 1740. Nudging 300 years old, it was hardly surprising that the doll's condition was a little worn. In reality, she was a very rare survivor and, to audible gasps from the audience, Fergus gave her an auction value of £20,000. The owner was also advised on how to preserve the doll and prevent her dress from further decay – some conservation work has been done on her since the show. The family has decided to keep and safeguard her for future generations.

# A MARIA HEATHCOTE PORTRAIT

For many years, the Furniture Round has been an integral part of the logistics associated with the *Roadshow* production. The service – moving large items to and from a venue – helps those unable to do it themselves and also varies the material appearing on the show. The skill for all those involved (including many experts who have taken part over the years) is to take away and return the items carefully without offering any clues as to why the show might be interested in them. In 2015, just before the show was due to take place at Bowood House (Wiltshire), expert Marc Allum's interest was piqued by a letter from a school in Devizes that had put forward some objects for appraisal, including a large portrait hanging in the school's reception area.

The main part of Devizes School is actually a large Georgian country house, originally known as Southbroom House. Dating from the 1770s, this was home to Maria Eyles, who inherited the house from her father, Edward. Aged around eighteen, she married George Heathcote, who was to become Lord Mayor of London in 1742. The full-length oil painting in question is of Maria Heathcote who, legend has it, still haunts the building. It was obvious that this elegant lady, who silently looked down on the children day after day, had a story to tell, so Marc arranged for her to be picked up by the carriers the day before the show.

Paintings expert Dendy Easton had the pleasure of assessing the painting on the day and was pleased to find himself with both the school's headmaster and a selection of pupils. Amusingly, a few spots on the picture turned out to be tissue pellets blown from pen tubes over the years – clearly the lady had been used as surreptitious target practice by mischievous pupils! Dendy examined the picture carefully and found that it was dated 1725 – the year after Maria's marriage to George Heathcote – and was signed by the artist, John Vanderbank. He was a painter of Huguenot descent who gained a reputation as a society painter during the reign of George I (1714–1727). Vanderbank had even studied under leading portraitist Sir Godfrey Kneller, but heavy drinking and a spell in debtor's prison took their toll on his health and he died of tuberculosis in his mid-forties.

As Dendy pointed out, in the portrait Maria can be seen holding an oyster shell, a symbol of fertility. Meaningful nuances such as these were typical of artworks of the period. Overall, the headmaster and the children were pleased to learn more about the lady with the ghostly reputation. Dendy valued Maria Heathcote's portrait at £10,000. Although this was pleasing, the lady was certainly not about to be sold. Marc made sure that she was safely returned to her

spot in the entrance hall the very next day. The school has since been busy raising money to have her cleaned and preserved, and when this happens it will be a good outcome for both the school and for Maria Heathcote.

# A WEIRD GLASS

*Roadshow* glass expert Andy McConnell has a bit of a reputation for the odd hi-jinks. Putting it bluntly, he likes to have a bit of fun with his contributors. At Chepstow racecourse in 2012, he did however, find himself with an object that was distinctly flummoxing. As Andy pointed out, '*Ninety-five per cent of the material that the specialists see on a* Roadshow *you take in your stride, but there's always going to be five per cent that leaves you scratching your head*'. This was one of those pieces – Andy came up with some interesting theories as to what exactly the unusual-looking glass construction might be. Comprising two creatures with open mouths over a bulbous reservoir with what appeared to be a 'reflecting' plate of some type, Andy went for the 'oil lamp' option. This seemed reasonable enough – but as Andy admitted, he was not entirely sure. Nonetheless, he valued it for £1,000 to £3,000. A follow-up appointment was accordingly arranged for the unusual-looking 'glass' to be taken to the Victoria & Albert Museum, which houses one of the greatest glass collections in the world. The owner had previously expressed an interest in donating the item to a museum, so this idea seemed like a win-win situation for both parties – assuming that the museum actually wanted it.

Neither was to be disappointed. Although unique in itself, the strange creation was in fact a puzzle or trick glass. Its uniqueness is actually encapsulated in its design, and also because it is a totally handmade object borne of the fanciful notions of the maker – a tricky piece for any glass blower to attempt. So, although a similar class of objects does exist, this was in fact a real rarity. As the museum curator explained to Andy, the 'glass' was Bohemian and the date of origin was quite early – around 1700–1750. The purpose of the outlandish object was literally to amaze and amuse guests. The curator speculated that filling the two reservoirs with water and wine and controlling the flow by placing two fingers over two holes on the reservoirs would allow a controllable release of liquid. Perhaps for the first time in 200 years, Andy actually attempted this particular trick – and it worked a treat.

A happy outcome for all was cemented. The owners did donate the item to the V&A and it now resides under museum number C.9-2012 in the glass collection, Room 131, case 11, shelf 2, where any visitor can happily go and see it. At this point, the value of the glass had become largely immaterial, as it now sits in a national collection. However, as Andy said '*the whole thing is just the complete package; it ends up where it should be*'.

# SPECIAL PROGRAMMES

*Antiques Roadshow* is an enduring and important part of our popular culture. It is referenced continually in all aspects of our everyday lives. Much loved, often satirised and continually surprising, it is both reliable, comfortable and yet able to pull the most astounding coups out of its Sunday evening reputation for being the calm before the storm of the week. Over the decades, this has been illustrated by its ability to adapt to the different demands of its varied audience. The show does this by supporting patriotic, Commonwealth and European aspects of our history and culture as well. As a result, we have seen the *Roadshow* take on emotionally challenging and difficult subjects, such as the Holocaust Memorial Special, which centred on the government's project to record the testimonies of the surviving Holocaust survivors and their liberators. It was a show that some said could not be made, but as the outpouring of emotion following the transmission showed, the mixture of grief, shock, horror and love that flowed through the media as a result of the brave nature of the contributors, exemplified the *Roadshow*'s ability to deal with tough subjects in a well-tested way. As David Baddiel said on his Twitter feed '*Completely emotionally destroyed by* #antiquesRoadshow. *That's a sentence I was never expecting to write*'. He was one of many who felt this way.

## AN EMOTIONAL ROLLERCOASTER

Such emotions have also been echoed in other *Roadshow* episodes, such as the 'Remembrance' and 'World War One' Specials from the National Memorial Arboretum and Somme Battlefields respectively. The raw emotion encapsulated in the tales of heroism and suffering brought about by the testimony of the owners, the power of the objects and the poignancy of the photographs, made half of the nation weep, as well as many of the experts participating on the shows. The letter from Teddy to his dear pregnant wife, a gunner killed in action when his Halifax bomber was shot down in World War Two, had Hilary Kay wiping away the tears, as were several million viewers, too. But such tales are not all about sadness – they are about resolve and spirit and, even though Teddy knew that the letter would be read after his death, he still wrote '*remember darling, unhappy moments often turn into happy ones, and never give up hope*'.

*Graham Lay, Martin Pegler, Paul Atterbury and Bill Harriman, four of the five experts who took part in the WW1 Special, filmed on the Somme in 2013. The fifth (not pictured here) was Hilary Kay.*

*During the WW1 Special Bill Harriman met the family of Thomas Halliwell at Warloy-Baillon cemetery in the Somme, for their first visit to his grave. Halliwell was killed on 2 October 1916.*

# ANTIQUES
# ROADSHOW
## THE NEXT GENERATION

Join Michael Aspel and Fearne Cotton from CBBC
for a special Antiques Roadshow for children
and young people under the age of 18.

# NATIONAL RAILWAY
# MUSEUM, YORK

## SUNDAY, 16th NOVEMBER, 2003

### FREE TICKETS

If you'd like to have your treasures evaluated by the experts,
write now for an application form enclosing a large SAE to:

**ANTIQUES ROADSHOW – THE NEXT GENERATION**
**PO BOX 229**
**BRISTOL BS99 7JN**

or fill in the website application form – **www.bbc.co.uk/antiques**

Background Image Courtesy of

**NRM**
NATIONAL
RAILWAY
MUSEUM

*Justin Pressland discusses a* Dr Who *collection at a* Children's Roadshow.

## AN OLD FRIEND

This ability to convey such emotional and powerful material is something that the *Roadshow* has – in a way – grown into. Although the show format has superficially changed very little, its subtle evolution has given it the ability to deal with all manner of stories in a very credible way. Objects are the catalysts behind these stories and, no matter how grand or humble, how incredibly well-made or naive an artefact might be, it fires the connective starting-pistol to history. *Roadshow* specialists are therefore required to be both experts and consummate story tellers, bringing history to life for the audience. As a tailor-made vehicle that brings innovation and variety to the *Roadshow*'s loyal following, Specials also attract new audiences. As result, the show has explored many different avenues over the years. The *Children's Roadshows*, specifically aimed at a younger audience, took place over some fourteen seasons – starting in 1992 – and featured many engaging locations such as the National Railway Museum in York and the British Motor Museum in Gaydon.

As well as utilising niche locations, such as the 2004 Special from HMS *Victory* and various compilations and anniversary shows, it has occasionally, gone completely off-piste and entered into the all-important national effort to raise money for major charitable

*The* Antiques Roadshow *came to Dibley in 2005, in support of* Comic Relief.

causes. In 2005, there was the 'Comic Relief Vicar of Dibley Special' and in 2007 a 'Sport Relief Special' was made at Lord's Cricket Ground. *Antiques Roadshow* also has an enormous foreign audience and is franchised all over the world. As a result, it has made several forays to foreign lands which have seen some of its biggest queues ever, accumulated in countries such as Canada where in 2001 it visited Ottawa and Toronto, and Australia, where in 2005 it visited Sydney and Melbourne. In Australia, there were over 20,000 applications for tickets. Other destinations have included Belgium, Sweden, Jamaica, Malta, Gibraltar and France. However, the underlying message of the *Roadshow* has always been rooted in a resolute Britishness, which has continually been reflected in its historic associations with the royal family.

*Her Majesty the Queen and Prince Philip enjoyed a private* Roadshow *in 2015 with Hilary Kay, Paul Atterbury and John Axford.*

## ROYAL ASSOCIATIONS

Accordingly, the 'Diamond Jubilee Special' at Kensington Palace featured a raft of personal stories and nostalgic recollections from contributors, including a piece of the Queen's Wedding Cake, valued at over £1,000 by Marc Allum. In 2014, Paul Atterbury, Hilary Kay and John Axford were honoured to meet Her Majesty and Prince Philip at their official residence in Northern Ireland, Hillsborough Castle, where they personally discussed several items with the royal couple. In 2015, a special show was filmed at Balmoral Castle as well, specifically to celebrate the Queen becoming Britain's longest-serving monarch. More recently, a special – filmed on the Royal Yacht *Britannia* – was finished for future transmission.

*Filming in the splendid setting of Melbourne's Exhibition Building during the* Roadshow's *visit to Australia.*

## UNRIVALLED VARIETY

As well as celebrating milestones in the show's history – this one included – special episodes have, in latter years, also utilised particular themes as vehicles for exploring certain areas of the art and antiques market. A 'Golden Age of Travel Special' was a first for the show in 2016 and featured a logistically difficult but ambitious transmission in which interesting items from the world of transport and travel were presented in conjunction with the United Kingdom's most famous locomotive, the *Flying Scotsman*, fresh from its ten-year restoration. A collection of air hostesses' outfits certainly broke the mould! Another special, recently finished in 2017, came from the set of *EastEnders*, the BBC's flagship drama, and showcased material from the world of entertainment, including objects such as Mike Oldfield's guitar and Darth Vader's helmet. Such is the diversity and opportunity that the show strives to offer to its viewers that the *Roadshow* will no doubt explore many other genres in the future. However, the United Kingdom, throughout its long history, additionally has had much to celebrate in its cultural diversity. This was strongly represented in the India Special of 2015, in which the art and culture of this great country were explored – not in India, but at the incredible BAPS Shri Swaminarayan Mandir, a Hindu temple in Neasden, London. This spectacular, towering marble edifice served as a wonderful backdrop to various Anglo-Indian tales and even included a Maharajah's Rolls-Royce. That is why the 'Special' is so very special to the ethos of the show.

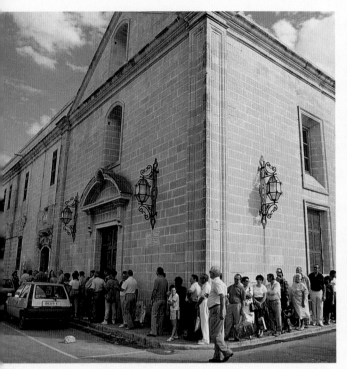

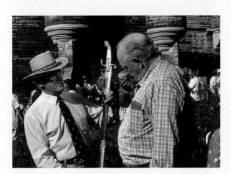

LEFT PAGE: *top left, the* Roadshow *in Malta; top right, the* Roadshow *in Sydney, Australia; centre, the* Holocaust Special; *bottom left, the* Children's Roadshow; *bottom right, the* Roadshow *in Ottawa, Canada.* RIGHT PAGE: *top left, the* Holocaust Special, *top right, the* Roadshow *in Kingston, Jamaica; centre, Casa Loma, Toronto, Canada; bottom, airline hostess uniforms on the Travel Special.*

# INDEX

Album of Filipino watercolours  36–7
*Alice in Wonderland*  294–5
Alma-Tadema portrait  86–9
Alma-Tadema, Sir Lawrence  86–9
Allum, Marc  96–7, 120–1, 128–31, 136–9,
   146–7, 190–1, 192–3, 198, 204–5, 207,
   244–5, 300–1, 210
Ambrose punch pot  262–3
Amundsen, Roald  72–3
Apothecary cabinet  232–3
Archdale, George  186–9, 203
Archer-Morgan, Ronnie  220–3
Arkwright, John  290
Arley Hall  88
Aberglasney House and Gardens  256
Art galleries
   Lefevre Gallery  288
   Tate  67
   The Lowry  289
*Art of the Old English Potter, The*  26
*Artist's Halt in the Desert, The* see Richard Dadd
   painting
Ashton Court  192–3, 240–3
Atterbury, Paul  16, 18–19, 78, 96–7, 106–9,
   123, 160, 310
Aubicq, Yvonne  52–5
Auction houses
   Christie's  36, 60, 67
   Phillips  26, 47
   Sotheby's  8, 103, 104, 139, 253
Audemars, Jules-Louis  184–5
Austen, Jane  276–7
Axford, John  256–7, 310
Audemars Piguet watch  184–5
Audley End  167

Baddeley, Jon  124–5
Baddiel, David  306
Balmoral Castle  313
Banksy lovers  240–3
BAPS Shri Swaminarayan Mandir (Neasden)  313
Barrett, Bryan  157
Battie, David  8, 15, 16, 18–19, 207, 252–5,
   262–3
Battle of Waterloo  62–3
Beatrix Potter drawings  114–17
Belton House  273
Benjamin, John  69, 171, 195
Bergman, Franz  90
Bett, Hugh  73–5
Beverley Minster  124
Biggs, Ronnie  202–3
Birchall, Thomas  33
Bizarre fishing rod  208–9
Blake, William  293
Blenheim Palace  294
Blue John  76–7

Bly, John  78, 174–5
Bodnant Gardens  20
Bolan, Marc  136–9
Bonaparte, Napoleon  62
Bowood House (Wiltshire)  300
Bowers, Birdie  73
Brittain, Penny  38
Bruce, Fiona  14, 56, 94, 154, 172–3, 249, 307
Boulton, Matthew  76
Bridgend Recreation Centre  129
Buffalo Bill gloves  82–3
Bull, Simon  8, 42–3, 192
Bull's head stirrup cups  290–1
Burdett, Edward  110–11
Burges brooch  154–5
Burges, William  16–19, 154–5
Business Design Centre  28–9
Butler, Roy  62–3, 268
Buxton Pavilion  76–7

Calkin James, Margaret  176–9
Campione, Bunny  198–9
*Carpathia* memorabilia  126–7
Carroll, Lewis  294–5
Cartier wristwatch  260–1
Cassandre, A. M.  118
Cato, Lennox  232
Cawdor Castle  78
Chartwell House  140
Chatsworth House  104
Chenies Manor  211
Chinese armorial dish  256–7
Christofle & Cie  210
Churchill cigar  56–7
Churchill, Winston  56–7, 140
Clarke, George  285
Cliveden House  171
Cody, William Frederick *see* Buffalo Bill gloves
Cold-painted bronze parrot  90–1
Comic Relief *Vicar of Dibley* Special  310
Conan Doyle, Sir Arthur  106–9
Cook, Captain James  123
Cottingley fairies  106–9
Cromwell's funeral flag  272–5
Coughton Court  176
Crawley silver, the  278–9
Credenza story, the  64–5
Crichton, Alexander  168
Crichton-Stuart, John, 3rd Marquess of Bute  16
Cromwell, Oliver  272–5
Curry, John  168

Dallin, Cyrus  20
Dadd, Richard  30–3
Dambusters' panda mascot  148–9
Dark Ages, The  164
Delftware Turk's head  44–7

Derngate Centre (Northampton)  24–7
Devizes School  300–1
Devonshire, Duchess of  104
Diamond butterfly brooch  194–5
Diamond Jubilee Special  310
Dickin, Maria  280
Dickin Medals  280–1
Dickinson, Alastair  290–1
Dobson, Frank  100
Dodgson, Charles Lutwidge  *see* Carroll, Lewis
Dolls' house  228–31
Drake, Robin  15
Dulwich College Picture Gallery  66–7
Dumphries House  114, 143

Early doll  298–9
*EastEnders* set  313
Easton, Dendy  300–1
Eighteenth-century dress  186–9
English marquetry commode  174–5
English Rose kitchen  244–5
Experts
   Allum, Marc  96–7, 120–1, 128–31, 136–9,
      146–7, 190–1, 192–3, 198, 204–5, 207,
      244–5, 300–1, 210
   Archdale, George  186–9, 203
   Archer-Morgan, Ronnie  220–3
   Atterbury, Paul  16, 18–19, 78, 96–7, 106–9,
      123, 160, 310
   Axford, John  256–7, 310
   Baddeley, Jon  124–5
   Battie, David  8, 15, 16, 18–19, 207, 252–5,
      262–3
   Benjamin, John  69, 171, 195
   Bett, Hugh  73–5
   Bly, John  78, 174–5
   Bull, Simon  8, 42–3, 192
   Butler, Roy  62–3, 268
   Campione, Bunny  198–9
   Cato, Lennox  232
   Dickinson, Alastair  290–1
   Easton, Dendy  300–1
   Farmer, Will  264–7
   Ford, Grant  218–19?
   Gambon, Fergus  228–31, 298
   Haley, Matthew  234–7
   Hardy, Joanna  166–7
   Higgins, Katherine  214–17
   Inglis, Brand  38–41
   Hook, Philip  8, 28–9, 134–5
   Kay, Hilary  60, 82, 96–7, 104, 111, 176–9,
      186–9, 205, 272–5, 306, 310
   Knowles, Eric  90, 142–3, 210–11
   Lambert, Deborah  181
   Graham Lay  248–51, 280–1, 282–5

Leatham, Victoria 98, 126
Lloyd, Lisa 118–9
Maas, Rupert 52–5, 67, 86–9, 240–3
Miller, Judith 226–7
Mould, Philip 93–5
Munn, Geoffrey 154–5, 164–5
Nahum, Peter 30–3, 36–7, 292–3
Negas, Arthur 8, 10
Payne, Christopher 20, 50–1, 78–81
Pickford, Ian 168, 278–9
Sandon, Harry 26–7
Sandon, John 45–7
Schoon, Adam 208–9
Smith, Mark 148–9
Somerville, Stephen 140, 288–9
Stewart-Lockhart, Clive 150–3
Tharp, Lars 200–1, 252–5
Viney, Paul 276–7
Exhibitions
    Manchester Art Treasures 33

Farahar, Clive 100–3, 114–17, 296–7
Farmer, Will 264–7
Farnborough Wind Tunnels 202
Farnham Sports Centre 42–3
Feuilles Fougeres see Lalique vase
Fiji bulibuli club 220–3
First World War 52–5, 185, 209, 306
Flaxman, John 268
Flying Scotsman, The 313
Fogelberg, Andrew 38
Ford, Grant 218–19
Fordsham mantel clock 258–9
Foster, John 156–9
Foster, Norman 244
Foujita painting 28–9
Foujita, Tsuguharu 28–9
Francis Souza painting 66–7
Frost, Terry 134

Gallery spreads 34–5, 84–5, 132–3, 162–3,
    182–3, 238–9, 314–15
Gambon, Fergus 228–31, 298
George Richmond miniature 292–3
Gibson, Tim 15
Graham Sutherland painting 140–1
Great Train Robbers' Monopoly set 202–3
Gregynog Hall 282
Golden Age of Travel Special 313
Goldsmiths' Hall 167
Griffiths, Frances 106–9

Haley, Matthew 234–7
Hallett, William 232
Hampton Court 81
Hampton Court Estate 290
Hanbury Hall 22–3, 208
Hardie, Will 285
Hardy, Joanna 166–7
Harland and Wolff shipyard (Belfast) 106
Harper, John 160
Hartland Abbey 150
Hawth, The 278
Healiss, Georgina 214–17
Heath, Adrian 134
Heathcote, Maria 300–1
Henry Moore letters 100–3
Hepworth, Barbara 100, 134
Hereford town hall 8–10
Higgins, Katherine 214–17

Hill Top Farm 115, 117
Hilton, Roger 134
Hiroshima Bowls 200–1
Hirst, John Henry 208–9
HMS Endeavour 122–3
HMS Victory 309
Holocaust Memorial Special 306
Hook, Philip 8, 26–7
Holkham Hall 82
Houghton Hall 164
Hurley, Frank 72

India Special 313
Indian painting 296–7
Inglis, Brand 38–41
In the First Garden see George Richmond miniature

Jane Austen cup-and-ball 276–7
Japanese POW caravan plans 282–5
Japonisme Gem 210–11
Jean Dupas posters 254–5

JFK's flying jacket 246–7
Kay, Hilary 60, 82, 96–7, 104, 111, 176–9,
    186–9, 205, 272–5, 306, 310
Kent, William 180–1
Keel of Endeavour 122–3
Kendall, Evelyn 100–3
Kennedy, President John F. 246–7
Kensington Palace 310
King Charles I 93, 273
King Charles II 98, 273, 279
Knowles, Eric 90, 142–3, 210–11
Kronborg Castle (Denmark) 252

Lalique vase 142–5
Lalique, René 142–5
Lambert, Deborah 181
Lawrence of Arabia watch 192–3
Lay, Graham 248–51, 280–1, 282–5
Leatham, Victoria 98, 126
Leica II Luxus camera 128–31
Lewis Carroll collection 294–5
Lewis, Christopher 15
Liddell, Alice 294
Lincoln Cathedral 56–7
Lindner portrait 218–19
Lindner, Richard 218–19
Lloyd, Lisa 118–9
Lloyd's Patriotic Fund sword 268–9
Lord's Cricket Ground 310
Lowenstam, Leopold 86–9
Lowry, L. S. 288–9
Lozano, José Honorato 36–7
Lozano, José Honorato Types and Costumes of the
    Philippines 36
Lulworth Castle 232

Maas, Rupert 52–5, 67, 86–9, 240–3
Marc Bolan's Gibson 'Flying V' guitar 136–9
Margaret James, poster designer 176–9
Maria Heathcote portrait 300–1
Märklin tinplate biplane 104–5
Martinware collection 264–7
Matchstick Men – L. S. Lowry painting 288–9
May the Force 286–7

McGee, Dr Edward 126
Medina Hall, Newport (Isle of Wight) 90
Menai Suspension Bridge 205

Miller, Glenn 150–3
Miller, Judith 226–7
Milton Manor 157, 159
Mintons 26
'Mobile Lovers' 240–3
Moore, Henry 100–3
Mortimer, John 38
Moss, Stirling 124
Mould, Philip 93–5, 134–5
Mount Stewart House (Northern Ireland) 198
Mughal bracelets 68–9
Munn, Geoffrey 154–5, 164–5
Museums & collections
    Bethlem Royal Hospital Museum 31
    British Museum 33
    British Motor Museum 309
    Calouste Gulbenkian Museum 143
    Glenn Miller Archives 153
    Henry Moore Foundation 103
    Imperial War Museum 55, 251, 280
    Jane Austen's House Museum 276
    Metropolitan Museum of Art 253
    Museum of Fine Arts (Boston) 20
    Museum of London 274
    National Army Museum 134
    National Railway Museum 309
    National Trust 117
    Omega Museum 193
    Potteries Museum 26
    Royal Collection, Windsor 41
    STEAM 298
    Thames Valley Police Museum 202
    Titanic Museum 160
    Victoria & Albert Museum 16, 31, 33, 81,
        117, 154, 178, 188,
    Virginia Museum of Fine Arts (US) 41

Nahum, Peter 30–3, 36–7, 292–3
National Memorial Arboretum 306
Negas, Arthur 8, 10
Newspaper posters 112–13
Newstead Abbey 93
North Devon Leisure Centre 30
Norwich Cathedral 201

Old Testament figures 252–3
Orpen, Sir William 52–5
Ozzy the owl 22–5

Palladio, Andrea 181
Paget, Henry first Marquess of Anglesey 204–5
Pankhurst, Emmeline 214
Parfitt, Rick 190–1
Parker, Bruce 13
Paul Storr salts 38–41
Payne, Christopher 20, 50–1, 78–81
Pembroke Castle 70–1
Phillips, Sir Thomas 30–1, 33
Pickford, Ian 168, 278–9
Piguet, Eduard-Auguste 184–5
Plane spotter's notebooks 150–3
Plas Newydd 204–5
Ponting, Herbert 72, 75
Pop Art 218
Post, Gunilla von 246–7
Potter, Beatrix 114–17
Presenters
    Bruce, Fiona 14, 56, 94, 154, 249, 307
    Parker, Bruce 13
    Rippon, Angela 10, 13

Scully, Hugh 8, 10–11, 13–14, 18
Prince Philip 310

Queen Anne dolls 229
Queen Anne travelling chest 78–81
Queen Elizabeth II 310
Queen Victoria 87, 290, 295, 298

RAF Coningsby 148
Ratcliffe, Flight Sergeant William Gordon 148–9
Reade, Paul 15
Refugee, The see William Orpen portrait
Refuse tip jewellery 170–1
Regency peat buckets 50–1
Remington, Frederick 20
Reiber, Emile Auguste 210
Renaissance gold plaque 42–3
Restoration, The 98, 158, 273
Richard Dadd painting 30–3
Richmond, George 292–3
Rippon, Angela 10, 13
RMS Carpathia 126–7
RMS Titanic 59–61, 106, 126, 160–1
Rommel's cigarette packet 248–51
Rommel, General Erwin 248–51
Remembrance Special 306
Roosevelt, President Theodore 59, 198
Rossi, Francis 190–1
Rostron, Captain Arthur Henry 126
Royal Agricultural University (Cirencester) 93
Royal Pigeon Racing Association 280
Royal Yacht Britannia 313
Rundell, Bridge & Rundell 38

Sainsbury Centre (University of East Anglia) 244
Salle de la Madeleine (Brussels) 36–7
Salisbury Cathedral 38–41
Salter's Company, The 41
Saxon gold ring 164–5
Schoon, Adam 208–9
Scott expedition photographs 72–5
Shakespeare notebook 234–7
Shaw, Simon 15
South Pole 72–5
Scrimshaw carvers 110–11
Sandon, Harry 26–7
Sandon, John 45–7
Scott, Captain Robert Falcon 72–5
Scully, Hugh 8, 10–11, 13–14, 18
Second World War 56–7, 134, 148–9, 150–3, 248–51, 280, 282–5, 306–7
Shackleton, Ernest 72
Silver duck claret jug 168–9
Sioux warrior by Dallin 20–21
Slipware pottery 24–7
Smith, Mark 148–9
Solon, L. M.
Somerville, Stephen 140, 288–9
Somme Battlefields 306
Souza, Francis Newton 66–7
Special programmes 306–13
Spirit of the Wind 143
Sprimont, Nicholas 41
Status Quo tapestry 190–1
Skegness Embassy Centre 16
Sport Relief Special 310

Staffordshire pottery 24–7
STEAM 298
Steiff, Margarete 59, 198
Steiff Clown bear 198–9
Steiff Titanic bear 58–61
Storr, Paul 38–41, 290
Stuart table casket 98–9
Stewart-Lockhart, Clive 150–3
Stump work box 156–9
Suffrage medal 214–17
Sunbeam-Talbot 90 Rally Car 124–5
Sutherland, Graham 140–1
Swansea Town Hall 136
Sydney University 59
Syon Park 100

Tale of Peter Rabbit, The see Beatrix Potter drawings 114–17
Telford, Thomas 205
Tenniel, John 295
Terry Frost portrait 134–5
Tewkesbury Abbey 187, 228
Tharp, Lars 200–1, 252–5
Theed, William 41
Thomas Telford gate 204–5
Titanic letter 160–1
Toft, Thomas 25
Tory loo seat 226–7
Tourmaline ring 166–7
Tredegar House 190, 248–51
Trentham Gardens 218

Vanderbank, John 300–1
Van Dyck portrait 92–5
Van Dyck, Sir Anthony 92–5
Venues
    Aberglasney House and Gardens 256
    Arley Hall 88
    Ashton Court 192–3, 240–3
    Belton House 273
    Balmoral Castle 313
    BAPS Shri Swaminarayan Mandir (Neasden) 313
    Beverley Minster 124
    Blenheim Palace 294
    Bodnant Gardens 20
    Bowood House (Wiltshire) 300
    Bridgend Recreation Centre 129
    British Motor Museum 309
    Business Design Centre 28–9
    Buxton Pavilion 76–7
    Cawdor Castle 78
    Chartwell House 140
    Chatsworth House 104
    Chenies Manor 211
    Cliveden House 171
    Coughton Court 176
    Derngate Centre (Northampton) 24–7
    Dulwich College Picture Gallery 66–7
    Dumphries House 114, 143
    EastEnders set 313
    Embassy Centre (Skegness) 16
    Farnham Sports Centre 42–3
    Farnborough Wind Tunnels 202
    Flying Scotsman, The 313
    Gregynog Hall 282

Hampton Court Estate 290
Hanbury Hall 22–3, 208
Harland and Wolff shipyard (Belfast) 106
Hartland Abbey 150
Hereford town hall 8–10
HMS Victory 309
Holkham Hall 82
Houghton Hall 164
Kensington Palace 310
Kronborg Castle (Denmark) 252
Lincoln Cathedral 56–7
Lord's Cricket Ground 310
Lulworth Castle 232
Medina Hall, Newport (Isle of Wight) 90
Melbourne Convention & Exhibition Centre 59–61
Mount Stewart House (Northern Ireland) 198
National Memorial Arboretum 306
National Railway Museum 309
Newstead Abbey 93
North Devon Leisure Centre 30–3
Norwich Cathedral 201
Pembroke Castle 70–1
Plas Newydd 204–5
RAF Coningsby 148
Royal Agricultural University (Cirencester) 93
Royal Yacht Britannia 313
Sainsbury Centre (University of East Anglia) 244
Salle de la Madeleine (Brussels) 36–7
Salisbury Cathedral 38–41
Somme Battlefields 306
STEAM 298
Swansea Town Hall 136
Sydney University 59
Syon Park 100
Tewkesbury Abbey 187, 228
Hawth, The 278
Tredegar House 190
Trentham Gardens 218
Victoria Hall 207
Walmer Castle 118, 246, 264
Whitchurch Leisure Centre 50–1
Audley End 167
Victoria Hall 207
Viney, Paul 276–7

Walmer Castle 118, 246, 264
Waterloo chest 62–3
Watteau, Antoine 186–9
Wedgwood, Josiah 262
Weird glass 302–3
Wellington, Duke of 62, 118, 204, 246
Wheaton, Lawrence 167
Whieldon, Thomas 262
Whitchurch Leisure Centre 50–1
William Burges bottle 16–19
William Kent style table 180–1
William Orpen portrait 52–5
'Winner, The' enamel advertising sign 118–19
World War I special 306

Yuan bronze vase 206–7

# PICTURE CREDITS

# ACKNOWLEDGEMENTS

We are eternally grateful to our numerous *Roadshow* colleagues – both past and present – for their friendship over many years. Without this camaraderie it would have been much harder to write the book, reliant as it is, upon decades of extraordinary stories and great memories. Much gratitude should also go to the hard-working crew, too numerous to mention but vital in making the show happen. They are the unsung heroes of the production.

While writing the book was relatively straightforward, finding the photographs to match the words proved to be very difficult. The bulk of the images ultimately came from BBC sources and thanks to technology, we were able to 'grab' pictures, which over the last ten years, have come from our pioneering use of high definition television (HD). Many came from our own personal collections but we also had to rely on the help of several private individuals to fill the gaps. The most important of these is John Dallimore, the *Roadshow*'s greatest fan and, as it turns out, the keeper of the unofficial *Roadshow* archive. Thanks to his long established habit of attending and photographing as many *Roadshows* as possible and ever-

*John Dallimore, the* Roadshow*'s superfan, and for many years the programme's dedicated but unofficial photographer.*

willing help, there are far fewer gaps in the book. Thanks for supplying us with important photos are also due to Hilary Kay, Vic Coppin and Adrian Gruzman.

We must also thank *Homes and Antiques* magazine who made their extensive archive available to us, which together with the numerous boxes of BBC material proved extremely helpful. Unfortunately, neither came with photographic credits and so we can only thank collectively all those who have photographed *Roadshow* days over many years.

Thanks too must go to Executive Producer Simon Shaw for deciding that a book was a necessary part of the *Roadshow*'s 40th anniversary and for persuading us to write it, despite the challenging, if not almost impossible schedule. Thanks are also due to our researcher Amina Hassam.

Working with our publishers, Williams Collins, has been an enjoyable experience, thanks to the support, enthusiasm and patience of Myles Archibald and Julia Koppitz.

Lastly, the *Roadshow* wouldn't exist if it weren't for the unerring interest and enthusiasm in what we do. Without the tens of thousands of visitors and fans who queue every year there would be no *Antiques Roadshow*. Thank you.

*Paul Atterbury and Marc Allum*
*August 2017*